The Year of the Greylag Goose

Konrad Lorenz
The Year of the Greylag Goose

Photographs by Sybille and Klaus Kalas

Translated by Robert Martin

A Helen and Kurt Wolff Book | Harcourt Brace Jovanovich | New York and London

Design by Dieter Vollendorf

Printed in Germany

This book was translated from the German *Das Jahr
der Graugans*, published by R. Piper & Co. Verlag in 1979.
It was originally published in 1978 in France by
Editions Stock, under the title *L'Année de l'oie cendrée*.

Library of Congress Cataloging in Publication Data

Lorenz, Konrad.
The year of the greylag goose.

Translation of Das Jahr der Graugans.
"A Helen and Kurt Wolff book."
1. Greylag goose—Behavior. 2. Birds—Behavior.
I. Title.
QL696.A52L6913   598.4'1   79-1834
ISBN 0-15-199737-3

First American edition

B C D E

Foreword

This is not a scientific book. It would be true to say that it grew out of the pleasure I take in my observations of living animals, but that is nothing unusual, since all my academic works have also originated in the same pleasure. The only way a scientist can make novel, unexpected discoveries is through observation free of any preconceived notions.

An experimenter in a laboratory who sets out to answer a question relating to nature starts with a ready-made supposition that he wishes to confirm or refute. However, that supposition must always be based on a previous observation—or, to put it another way, on a subconscious cognitive process, involving the cooperation of the sense organs and the central nervous system, that converts sensory information into *perception*. It is vastly overestimating human powers of reasoning for a scientist to imagine that he already knows all the questions that can be asked about nature. If the scientist is thinking up his questions while confined to the laboratory and shut away from the infinite variety of living nature, it is all too easy for the questions to miss the really important issues and only turn up irrelevant matters. This often leads to incredibly penetrating and detailed investigations, to be sure, but may have little bearing on anything of real significance in the living world—though the research worker who has invested so much in the investigations is unable to understand that.

Whenever I sit for a couple of hours on the gravel bank of the river Alm with my flock of geese, or in front of my capacious aquarium of tropical fish at home in Altenberg, the time rarely goes by without my observing something unexpected. I never have an explanation at hand for these novel observations; rather, they lead me on to *new questions*, which require further observations and, very frequently, also experimental investigation. Ethologists like me do not conduct fewer experiments than the adherents of other schools of behavioral research; the difference is that we investigate only questions that arise from actual observation of animals, if possible in their natural environment.

Pure and simple observation provides the basis for all the

research we refer to as ethological. Just as the *description* of body parts is the foundation for comparative anatomy and morphology, the description of behavior patterns is the basis for comparative behavioral research, or *ethology*. In any kind of descriptive study, whether it deals with the spatial arrangement of organic structures or with the temporal patterning of movement in a living organism, our perceptual mechanisms play an important part. Such study thus involves a genuine cognitive process that underlies all our scientific knowledge. However, since the process takes place at a subconscious level and is inaccessible to introspection, it is *mistrusted* by research workers who place too much faith in rational thought. They will not concede that their own hypotheses, and the questions they tackle experimentally, depend on that same perceptual process. The contempt for the descriptive sciences that is so widespread today can be attributed to this very denial of perception as the source of scientific knowledge—a denial that has been elevated almost to the status of a religion.

It is possible that perception is treated with suspicion by some scientists—those who wish to keep their research "free of value judgments" at all costs—simply because perception is inseparable from sensations of beauty. It is a common error, but a pernicious one, to think that only what is gray and boring can be "scientific." Of the biologists who have really made outstanding contributions, there are only a handful who were not led to the subject of their lifework under the spell of its beauty. In my view, there is not one outstanding ethologist to whom that does not apply! A special gift for observation is virtually identical with a talent for perception, and indivisible from a hypersensitivity to the beauty of living organisms.

The harmony inhabiting all living things is what attracts our interest, and it would be utterly unscientific, if not downright dishonest, to deny this. A strictly objective description or illustration of an animal or plant departs from the truth in one crucial respect if the beauty of the living organism itself is not made evident. Of course, when we describe or illustrate the form of a bone, a fish's fin, or a bird's wing, we do not deliberately set out to express the beauty of the structure. We must not make the slightest departure from reality merely because our purely aesthetic sense of beauty leads us that way. On the other hand, our portrayal would not be quite faithful to reality if it did not also express the inherent beauty of the original.

After all, the beauty of the organic world emerges from that most objective of all representations, which owes nothing whatsoever to human perception, inevitably tinged with sentiment, but derives from an obviously soulless mechanical instrument—the camera! The lens of the camera, also technically known as the *objective*, is the very symbol of objectivity. In two other common optical instruments, the microscope and the astronomical telescope, the light rays bearing the image emerge from one end through the eyepiece, the part closest to the eye. To use an analogy, if the term "objective" is given to the main lens, the eyepiece could be called the "subjective," since the light rays coming from it must be converted by the human eye into an image on the retina. By contrast, the lens (or objective) of the camera transfers the light rays onto the light-sensitive surface of a layer of film, which objectively records the image. That image represents objective reality in the strictest sense of the word—the image would be exactly the same if it were never seen by the human eye.

No wonder, then, that the camera has become an indispensable instrument in numerous branches of objective science, and nowhere is it more important than in the field of comparative behavioral research. In other descriptive sciences it is possible to maintain a permanent record without the use of photography. In comparative morphology, one can take measurements and record dimensions and angles; in comparative anatomy, the specimen can be preserved as an objective record. But in comparative behavioral research, in which it is necessary to describe various patterns of movement, record them, and, above all, render them unmistakably recognizable, photography and cinematography provide the only means of objective documentation available—perhaps assisted by the tape recorder, which is becoming increasingly important.

An ethologist must learn how to take still photographs and

movies for the same reasons that an anatomist must master the techniques of preservation and dissection, or the histologist the techniques of staining and cutting sections with a microtome. All my students are more accomplished photographers than I am, though not all have achieved the same mastery as Sybille and Klaus Kalas. And no one has carried a heavy camera around more faithfully than Sybille Kalas: wherever she is, the camera is there, too. In theory, the cine-camera ought to be preferable for the recording of behavior patterns, but for the ethologist's practical day-to-day work the still camera is almost as good, provided that the photographer knows exactly what parts of a movement must be recorded for detailed analysis and that the camera can take photographs at sufficiently brief time intervals. Movies, which require considerable preparation, cannot be made as spontaneously, and, above all, it is impossible to carry even the smallest sixteen-millimeter camera in constant readiness while following animal subjects—something that can be done with a still camera.

Sybille Kalas has taken innumerable photographs of greylag geese for purely scientific purposes. In doing so, she was directing her attention not to the beauty of the subject, the artistic value of the angle, or the aesthetic quality of the light, but exclusively to the exact recording and replication of instantaneous behavioral events. Nevertheless, her pictures of greylag geese are outstandingly beautiful. Nature *is* beautiful and needs no artistic contribution to make it so.

None of the photographs published in this book was taken with that aim in mind. On winter evenings (which can seem very long in the Alm Valley), while working on our scientific evaluations of the pictures, we were struck time and again by their beauty, and the projector enabled us to relive the splendid hours we had passed in taking them. The time sequence of the pictures guaranteed that we could follow the annual cycle, just as we had experienced it with our geese. Every photograph brought forth our comments and reminiscences, and although our discussions were first and foremost scientific, we could not fail to appreciate that the pictures would undoubtedly be beautiful and interesting to the layman as well. That is how the plan for this book took shape. The impetus that led to its actual production was a suggestion from Editions Stock, our original publisher.

As I have said, this is not a scientific work, but a kind of by-product of our scientific research. That alone should demonstrate how beautiful objective truth can be, without retouching, when it is concerned with nature.

One final point: The book was an accomplished fact before I began to write the text. After all, its plan was predetermined in every detail by the photographs. At the turn of the century, Fritz von Ostini, a German poet whose name has sadly passed almost into oblivion, wrote the text for a delightful picture book of children's fairy tales compiled by the painter Hans Pellar. He wrote, "Here it is the poet who provides the illustration; the tales have been told by the painter." In this book there is exactly the same relationship between the text and the pictures.

When I retired as director of the Max Planck Institute for Behavioral Physiology, located on Lake Ess near Starnberg in Bavaria, my investigations into the social behavior of the greylag goose (*Anser anser* Linnaeus) were still in full swing. To enable me to continue the project, the Max Planck Society for the Promotion of Science set up a research station for me at my ancestral home in Austria, which was originally intended only for the goose project. The society's generous action is gratefully acknowledged here. Thanks are also due to the Cumberland Foundation (Cumberland-Stiftung), in particular to His Royal Highness Prince Ernst August von Cumberland and to the president of the foundation, Karl Hüthmayer. As a scientific institute the research station is affiliated with the Institute for Comparative Behavioral Research of the Austrian Academy of Sciences, and its official designation is Department 4, Animal Sociology.

The location and the particular form of the goose research station were made possible through the kind cooperation of the Cumberland Foundation. The Alm Valley of Austria is an area left virtually unscathed by the curse of modern technology. It begins at Lake Alm (2), which lies at the foot of the "Dead Mountain" and is the source of the narrow and rapidly flowing river Alm. About five miles downstream, at a point where the river valley broadens, Herr Hüthmayer had a number of ponds (1) dug out, surrounding sizable islands on which the geese are able to breed undisturbed. These artificial ponds are in complete harmony with the fairy-tale beauty of the surrounding countryside, and they are exclusively reserved for our research. Alongside the ponds are three small, heated huts in which the staff responsible for the care of the geese stays during the summer months. For this small settlement of geese and humans we have coined the name Oberganslbach (literally, "Upper Goose Stream").

Some miles farther downstream is the actual research-station building, a delightful old mill called Auingerhof, which the Cumberland Foundation rents to the Max Planck Society for a nominal fee and which the foundation has outfitted with all the facilities a research institute needs: darkroom, office, animal rooms, and so

2
From the "upper," or southwestern, shore one has an almost uninterrupted view of Lake Alm and can see just where the geese happen to be. When we are not using the boat, we can call the geese to us on the shore.

12

3
The institute is housed in the Auinger-hof, constructed in 1776. This old building, at one time linked to a millrace, lies between two streams on the shore of Lake Alm. The geese can often be found on the gravel flats bordering this part of the lake.

4
These young greylag geese were hand-reared at the institute and slept in their foster mothers' bedrooms in the first weeks after hatching. For this reason they often returned to the building even after fledging. It is apparent how relaxed and confident they feel as they preen themselves and settle down to rest in the doorway.

5

Wild boar can also be tempted with tidbits, particularly when provided by a human companion.

6

These two young wild boar are completely tame and on long walks follow their keeper, Michael Martys, like puppies. They are also tame toward other human beings, but they unerringly recognize their own keeper.

7

It is well known that young beavers often fall asleep while sucking on the mother's teat. This hand-reared beaver, Fritz, also liked to fall asleep holding a teat, in this case that of his nursing bottle.

on. The experimental animals wander freely in and out of the converted mill (3, 4).

The extent of untouched woodland and waterscape available to us allowed us to expand our research to include some large mammals living in their natural environment. The higher the organizational level of an animal species, the more sensitive its social life is to disturbances caused by an unnatural environment, especially those produced by close confinement. Such disturbances can, at least to some extent, be avoided by applying to mammals the same method we use with geese—observing *tame*, hand-reared individuals that are permitted complete freedom. We selected two mammal species that appeared to be promising subjects for behavioral research because of their well-developed social life and because of instinctive patterns that were of particular interest: the wild boar (*Sus scrofa*) and the beaver (*Castor fiber* Linnaeus).

As with the geese, it was necessary to build up tame, free-living populations of the two mammal species before their social behavior could be studied in the natural habitat. One must begin by hand-rearing young animals, which reorient their infant drives toward the human foster parent. Our wild boar have done so with their keeper, Michael Martys, and follow him through the woods like faithful dogs (5, 6). Wild boar are bred in large numbers in the Cumberland Foundation Wildlife Park, and piglets are available for our research whenever we require them. Wild boar are counted among the animal species, such as geese and dogs, that undertake large-scale migratory movements and therefore share strong bonds with their parents, which move ahead of them.

It is a different matter with beavers. They occasionally move outside their usual home range if conditions become unfavorable, as, for example, when their plant foods have been overgrazed. Thus, one cannot be sure, even with tame animals, whether the particular area in which they have been brought up will be to their liking, regardless of how much has been done to render them tame and attached to their foster parents. In addition, young beavers are not so easy to obtain or to hand-rear as boar piglets. Klaus Kalas had to experiment a great deal before he found the right milk formula.

8

In front of their artificial burrow, three tame hand-reared beavers, Laurie, Muck, and Hektor, are pampered with pieces of carrot from their foster parent, Klaus Kalas.

9

Although young hares are by no means easy to rear, we were successful on a number of occasions by using a mixture of baby milk powder and camomile tea. This is one of five young hares that were hand-reared at one of our goose huts in Oberganslbach and that remained nearby long after they became independent. They would amuse themselves by leaping across the meadow in a zigzag pattern over the sleeping geese.

Our study of the beaver has a double purpose, research and nature conservation. In the first place, an investigation into the social cooperation of beavers in relation to their well-known dam-construction activities promises to yield fascinating results. As far as is known to date, even the largest of beaver dams, which can raise the water level by about six feet and are over three hundred feet long, are the product of a single family (or a sequence of families). If that holds true, these animals must work for years on end, displaying the kind of industry for which their name is famous. Dam construction is of additional interest to behavioral researchers because it is almost exclusively based on inherited, instinctive activities and responses.

The conservation aspect of the project is of interest because the beaver is an almost extinct species in Central Europe, and its successful reintroduction would be extremely worthwhile (7, 8). For the time being, we have done no more than liberate a few naturally reared beavers in the wild. We do not yet dare risk this with hand-reared animals, and we intend to build up a fairly large tame population before attempting it. There is another reason we need a tame beaver population for our research: wild beavers are timid and will not emerge from their dens until late in the evening. This nocturnal activity is apparently determined by the nature of threats from their surroundings, since our tame beavers come out of their dens at one o'clock in the afternoon.

Sometimes we find ourselves hand-rearing other animals as well, mostly orphans that are brought to us from time to time—leverets in particular. We hand-rear these orphans and then release them in the wild carefully and progressively. Several hares we released that way proved to be unexpectedly intelligent and playful creatures. They remained in the neighborhood a long time and only slowly became independent of our feeding. Young hares do not retain contact with their real mothers so long and are weaned well before reaching the age of the tame hare in the picture (9).

Eventually, we hope to be able to report in more detail on the wild boar and the beaver in two separate books.

15

For the present, the most important subject of research at our field station is the greylag goose (10), which for many years has been at the center of my interests. Greylag geese generally inhabit the northern regions of Europe and Asia. The nearest local population is that of Lake Neusiedler, east of Vienna.

As a rule, greylag geese are migratory birds, although there are unusual, nonmigratory populations in Scotland. The path a population follows on its southward route in the autumn appears to be not innate but learned from generation to generation. Hand-reared geese, since their foster parents are unable to show them the path of autumn migration, stay with them at the place where they were reared.

I am often asked why we have made the greylag goose the subject of such extensive studies. There are many reasons, but the most important is that greylag geese exhibit a family existence that is analogous in many significant ways to human family life. I hasten to add that this is not an opinion based on anthropomorphization; we have discovered quite objectively, and not without a certain element of surprise, that pair formation ("marriage") among greylag geese follows almost exactly the same course as with ourselves. The young male exhibits a sudden infatuation for a particular young female, followed by intensive courtship of her—sometimes with considerable interference from an angry father. His courtship is in many details almost laughably similar to that of the young human male. The young gander shows off his strength and courage; he will attempt to attack and drive off other ganders, even those he is normally afraid of—though only when the object of his courtship is watching. In her presence he makes a great show of his physical strength. He will take to the air to cover a short distance that any noninfatuated goose would reasonably tackle on foot. Furthermore, he accelerates his takeoff more sharply than any "normal" goose would and brakes equally sharply when landing alongside his girl-friend. In this respect, he is behaving just like a young man on a motorcycle or in a sports car. If the female responds to his courtship, the two greylags perform a partnership ceremony, the so-called

10
The gander Greif follows our boat as we try to find Susi and her nest on Lake Alm. He assumes a deliberate air of indifference as we near the nest, so as not to betray his brooding consort.

18

triumph-calling ceremony. Then, if nothing intervenes, the two geese subsequently remain faithful to each other for the rest of their lives.

As we shall see, there are times when something does intervene, again just as with human beings.

A strong bond between the members of a greylag pair is forged by their joint love for their offspring, which on their part are equally loyal to their parents. If, during a breeding season, a pair of greylag geese lose their clutch or their goslings, their young from the previous year will usually return to them, unless the young are already "engaged." A goose that has lost its partner will return in the same way to rejoin either its parents or its still unpaired siblings. In short, the social behavior of greylag geese contains a great deal that is of interest to us, besides presenting us with a number of puzzles.

There is, however, one outstanding feature that makes the social behavior of the greylag goose especially suitable as a subject for ethological study: greylag geese that are reared from the egg under human care transfer to the human foster parent the loyal attachment they would display toward their real parents under natural conditions. It may sound sentimental, but it is an observable fact that our greylag geese remain attached to the area in which we want them to stay largely because of their lasting friendship with particular people.

The Alm Valley, where we decided to establish our new goose settlement, is in one respect extremely favorable for a goose population that will not be migrating southward in the autumn. Lake Alm is fed by artesian springs originating deep in the rock, and even in winter these are so warm that the lake never freezes over. The ponds of the Cumberland Foundation Wildlife Park and our own ponds at Oberganslbach are fed by water trickling through deep gravel beds from the river Alm. Hence, the ponds remain free of ice in the winter.

A less favorable factor is that the Alm Valley is a narrow mountain cleft, and the open grazing areas the geese require are found only in the immediate neighborhood of Oberganslbach, around Lake Alm itself, and in the area surrounding the research station at the Auingerhof mill. The geese have now learned to use the three areas preferentially, and they move methodically from one to another.

It was no easy matter to transfer the greylag goose colony from the Max Planck Institute on Lake Ess in Bavaria, where it was firmly established, to the new site in Austria. The story of the transfer is interesting in itself. To move the geese from Seewiesen, in Bavaria, to Grünau, in the Alm Valley, we made use of their attachment to their foster parents. In the spring of 1973, we had four willing goose foster parents, three girls and a young man, each ready to lead a flock of geese. They had to start the move in April, when the greylag goose eggs began to hatch. The foster children had to reach the Alm Valley before they fledged, since for every bird home is where it first takes to the air and explores its surroundings on the wing. This in turn fixed the time for the transfer of the first geese to Austria; it had to take place before the end of June. Our huts alongside the ponds were not yet prepared, however, and our goose "mothers" heroically put up with camping out in a game-feeding shed whose sidewalls consisted only of latticework. Wind and mist penetrated the shed with ease, as did the rain when the wind blew strongly. Even in June there is plenty of wind, mist, and rain in the Alm Valley!

Along with the four flocks of hand-reared young geese from that year, we transferred several groups of geese from the previous year that had been hand-reared by the same foster parents twelve months before and were therefore reliably attached to them. We also took along a number of goose families with youngsters that had not yet begun to fly, since we were reasonably sure that in the interests of their offspring they would not attempt to escape. At first all the birds were accommodated in a large aviary belonging to the Cumberland Foundation, situated alongside a pond inside the Wildlife Park about two-thirds of a mile downstream from our game-feeding point. But we encountered difficulties when we released them a few days later. The geese that had been hand-reared the year before immediately attached themselves to their foster parents and remained with them, while the families with youngsters wandered far and wide, in an attempt to move off, and had to be driven back to the large pond every evening in a strenuous herding operation. This operation was necessary because the pond offered the only security from the many foxes that inhabit the valley. Gradually, even these geese came to trust the human foster parents, and they moved from the aviary pond to the game-feeding site, which represented the initial center of our new goose colony.

When all the adult geese were able to fly again following the molt, they began to explore their surroundings together with the young geese of that year, which also had begun to fly. By autumn they were so well settled that when their human companions moved into the institute building they automatically went along, staying close to the house and seeking out the larger ponds—particularly Lake Alm—to pass the night. This behavior has since become a tradition. In summer the huts by our ponds are the center of the goose colony; in winter it is the Auingerhof mill building. On a fine autumn day the geese will abruptly appear outside the mill, sometimes before their human companions have moved in. But they will remain there only when the staff is in residence.

After the first heavy snowfall at the beginning of winter the geese avoid the meadows. They prefer to take no chances on falling into deep snow, from which takeoff would be difficult, and they tend to stay on the snow-free gravel banks bordering the river Alm.

At this time of year they pass the night on the great expanse of Lake Alm, where they are safe from foxes, and every morning after sunrise they come flying down the valley from the lake. The lake lies at a distance of about five miles from the Auingerhof mill and more than three hundred feet higher; the geese stay at the height of their takeoff point during this morning flight. Frequently they rise still higher in the sky. The many upcurrents that prevail in this mountainous area give them the opportunity to climb to

considerable heights without exerting themselves, and they obviously enjoy doing so. They can also give vent to the migratory urge that spurs them in autumn and spring by flying high and wide over the snow-covered mountains (11), before landing beside us on the gravel banks near the station building.

Even after having seen it so many times, I always find it utterly enthralling to witness free-flying birds moving toward me from a long distance away. After all, most poor (or perhaps wicked) souls never see wild animals except *from behind!* In all the lands of the earth where man has come in contact with wild animals, he is recognized as the most dangerous and merciless predator of all. There is hardly an animal, no matter how big and strong or how effective its weapons, that will not flee when it sees a human being approach. Only in places where man is unknown will the local animals approach him with complete trust, although usually this is utterly misplaced. One must travel to the Galapagos Islands or Antarctica to find animals that can be approached to within a few feet without being provoked to run or fly away.

Anyone who comes upon a large mammal in a wood will be greeted for a fraction of a second by a terrified animal face. Almost all its surface is taken up by sense organs: large, erect ears, widely staring eyes, and flaring nostrils. An instant later there is usually nothing to see but swaying branches, or at the most a rapidly disappearing view of the animal's rear. Birds, particularly the larger kinds, such as raptors, members of the crow family, and water birds, are if anything even shyer than mammals in the wild. In order to see them close up—and to take photographs—one must make use of the cunning techniques of hunters, either approaching very stealthily or constructing a well-camouflaged hide in a suitable place.

Man regards himself as Lord of the Earth, and so he is, though regrettably so in the sense just indicated, and then only on dry land. I remember quite clearly an occasion when I naïvely tried to chase off a barracuda, which simply adopted a threat posture and bared its teeth. That gave me the opportunity to find out just how fast one can swim backward with flippers!

Apart from such unwelcome exceptions, man cannot closely
approach free-living animals without causing them to take flight.
He has been exiled from the paradise of peaceful coexistence with
his fellow creatures. That is why, when free-living animals
approach me from a long distance away, not because they have
failed to notice me but for the very reason that they *have* seen me
and *have* heard me, it is as if this exile from paradise had been
lifted.

I am standing at a place in the Alm Valley where we sometimes
have a rendezvous with the geese. It is early morning; the mountain
peaks are partly lit by the sun, while the valley still bears the
grayness of dawn. Just above the spot where I am standing is a
layer of cloud. Then I hear, high in the air over my head, the calls
of geese flying by. I call out an answer, which evokes further calling
in response. In fact, I can recognize the call of a snow goose. At one
time we had with us a single female snow goose known as Arco,
who unfortunately has since preferred to return to the Max Planck
Institute, in Seewiesen. On the day in question, Arco was still with
us in the Alm Valley and had joined the greylag geese in their morning flight. I had barely heard her call when I saw her through a
small blue hole in the cloud layer, highlighted by the sun and
shining like a white star high in the sky. A moment later she had disappeared again behind the clouds, but she had heard me, and I
noticed from a small movement of her head that she had seen me as
well. A few seconds later the white bird plummeted through the
clouds and landed close by. Meanwhile, the greylag geese flew
farther down the valley until they reached the end of the clouds,
dropped downward, and flew back toward me underneath the cloud
cover.

Now, in the autumn, as I write these words, a multitude of
geese come flying back to the Auingerhof mill every morning from
Lake Alm, where they have spent the night. They plummet down
from a great height in the sky and land on the meadow in front of
the house. This happens as surely as day follows night, and in the
meadow we have constructed a comfortable bench and table on the
best spot for observing the geese. Whenever I am in Grünau I sit

13
When the sun climbs above the mountain on bitterly cold winter days, a veil of mist forms over the relatively warm water of Lake Alm. On such days the geese remain standing in the water to keep their feet warm.

14
When the geese come to eat on the shore of the lake, they settle down at once to warm their feet in their flank feathers. If they have just taken baths, as is the case here with the hand-reared gander Nils, water droplets immediately freeze on their feathers and are removed by nibbling movements of the beak.

there and wait for them every morning. Each time, their arrival brings me the same pleasure and the same sense of wonder, as their wing beats die away and they glide downward (12) before turning into a sharp dive and landing right next to us.

Even in the coldest weather the geese remain faithful not only to this particular place but also to their specific habits. The low temperature does not bother them (13), since, as I have said, the water remains well above freezing throughout the winter. The river gives off "steam" on cold days, and this water vapor condenses on trees and bushes along the banks to form delightful patterns of hoarfrost. If the sun comes out, sights of bewitching beauty are produced. When there is heavy frost, the geese will often stand in the relatively warm water. They remove the small beads of ice that sometimes form on their head feathers by taking baths (14).

Nowhere is spring as beautiful as it is in the Alps. The carpet of snow is replaced almost overnight by an array of flowers. As soon as a few snow-free patches have formed, one can find Christmas rose (*Helleborus niger* Linnaeus, 15), the remarkable flowers of the bog rhubarb (*Petasites hybridus* Linnaeus, 16), and the tender blossoms of the purple crocus (*Crocus albiflorus* Linnaeus, 17).

The geese also show signs of the awakening spring—the time of love. Young geese begin to split off from their family groups, partly under their own steam but also partly because their parents are preparing to breed again and no longer want the grown-up offspring around. Newly independent young ganders now carefully approach their chosen ones and adopt a characteristic posture of the body and neck, projecting the neck rigidly forward and downward (18).

After a young male has persisted in this form of courtship, often with great patience, over a number of days, he begins to grow somewhat more intimate and will direct the so-called triumph call at his prospective mate. He approaches her with his neck extended well out in front of him and utters a distinct gabbling call. Often this particular token of affection is immediately preceded by a mild

15
Even in December and January one can find buds of the Christmas rose (Helleborus niger L.), particularly on the southern slopes of Lake Alm. Their magnificent flowers break forth as soon as snow-free patches form in late winter and early spring.

16
The bog rhubarb (Petasites hybridus L.) also flowers early, its inflorescence sprouting from the ground vegetation even before the emergence of the leaves, which become so conspicuous in summer and autumn.

17
At about the same time one can find the fragile flower cups of the purple crocus (Crocus albiflorus L.), sometimes numbering in the thousands on the meadows.

attack the gander directs at another greylag goose. An observer cannot escape the sense that the gander is attempting to impress the object of his courtship with a display of courage (19).

At first the female will not respond to this sign of affection; in fact, she appears rather afraid of the gander. After a while, however, she begins—first shyly and then with increasing zest—to join in the calling of the gander. As soon as she does so, the "engagement" can be regarded as concluded. Provided that no dramatic circumstances intervene, a greylag goose pair formed in this manner will remain faithful for life. The greeting ceremony just described will be exhibited again, particularly when the pair are reunited after a major upheaval, following a long separation, for example, or after a stirring flight with other geese. The greater the excitation, the more intensive the calling will be. That is why Oskar Heinroth coined the term "triumph calling" to describe it (20).

Greylag goose pairs generally remain faithfully united until death. However, one of the "dramatic circumstances" that can intervene is the case of a gander or a goose abruptly and passionately "falling in love" with a different partner, despite a preexisting "engagement" or even a complete pairing. Such infidelity usually occurs only when something has been amiss in the original pair formation, for example when a gander has lost his first great love and has acquired his present partner as a substitute. In our many years of observing geese, there have been only three occasions on which we have witnessed the splitting up of a pair that had bred and successfully reared young. Remarkably, in two of these instances the seducer was the same gander, Ado.

Two geese hand-reared by different foster parents and bearing their surnames, according to our custom, the gander Janos Fröhlich and the female goose Susanne-Elisabeth Breit, had paired off and subsequently bred successfully in the spring of 1973. This pair was transferred with one offspring to Grünau, but in the autumn of 1973 all three flew off, and the parents returned alone in the spring of 1974. In the confusion of the move to Austria, the older and more powerfully built gander Ado had lost his "wife"—or, rather, his "bride," since they had not yet bred together. Janos was much

18
The geese begin their courtship on warm, sunny days of very early spring. This picture shows an old gander walking around his chosen mate with his neck held at a characteristic angle. The fluted contours of his neck feathers are clearly visible. At this time the beak and legs have a luminous red coloration.

19
The gander Traun, just returned from a three-year sojourn alone on Lake Traun, almost twenty miles away, performs a triumph call for the benefit of the female Lucia. This young female, recently separated from her family group, is still timid and gives no response.

weaker than Ado and was unable to prevent the unfaithful Susanne-Elisabeth from defecting in her passion for Ado. In 1976 Ado and Susanne-Elisabeth were breeding on Lake Alm when fate again took a hand, in the shape of a fox. One fine morning we found the lower part of Susanne-Elisabeth's body on the empty nest, with a deeply saddened Ado standing dumbstruck nearby.

Geese possess a veritably human capacity for grief—and I will not accept that it is inadmissible anthropomorphism to say so. Agreed, one cannot look into the soul of a goose, and the animal can hardly give us a verbal report of its feelings. But the same is true of the human child, and nevertheless John Bowlby, in his famous work on infant grief, has shown in a convincing and perturbing fashion how intensely small children can grieve. In all likelihood, their grief is deeper and more powerful than that of adults, because they are not yet able to find comfort in rational considerations. A dog whose master has gone away on a trip grieves as if the master were gone forever; the master cannot explain to the dog that he will return in a week. Dogs that have been left for long periods of time suffer such emotional harm that they are unable to respond with complete happiness when the master returns. Often, many weeks elapse before such a dog regains its former liveliness, and it may never do so. In terms of emotions, animals are much more akin to us than is generally assumed. It is in the capacity for rational thought that the enormous gulf between humans and animals exists. In my lectures and in my conversations with laymen, I frequently say, "Animals are much less intelligent than you are inclined to think, but in their feelings and emotions they are far less different from us than you assume."

That opinion is supported by what we know about the structure and function of the various parts of the brain. In human beings, as in animals, the capacity for rational intelligence is located in the forebrain (telencephalon), and the emotional center is located in the more basal areas of the brain. These basal areas in man are not essentially different from those in the brains of the higher animals; however, there is a correspondingly enormous difference in the degree of development of the cerebral hemispheres in the forebrain.

20
Even with pairs that have been established for many years, as with Selma and Gurnemanz in this picture, the female often fails to give an intensive response to her gander's triumph calling. However, in contrast to young pairs, such a gander can approach very close to his consort while calling and may even touch her.

21
After driving off his rival, Ado, seen here standing in the background, Gurnemanz returns to Selma and utters a triumph call. Selma attempts to join Ado, but Gurnemanz repeatedly blocks her way. The "cowed," withdrawn posture of her neck betrays Selma's uncertainty.

22
As he approaches Selma during his triumph call, Gurnemanz is so aroused that he actually bites her. Again Ado can be seen in the background, his neck held up in a demonstrative display.

The objective, physiological symptoms of deep emotion, especially grief, are virtually the same in humans as in animals, particularly geese and dogs. In the vegetative nervous system, the tonus of the sympathetic system declines, while that of the parasympathetic system (especially the vagus nerve) increases. As a consequence, the general excitability of the central nervous system is reduced, the musculature shows a decline in resilience, and the eyes sink deep into their orbits. Quite literally, a man, a dog, and a goose hang their heads, lose their appetites, and become indifferent to all stimuli emanating from the environment. For grief-stricken human beings, as well as for geese, one effect is that they become outstandingly vulnerable to accidents. Just as the former tend to become easy victims of car accidents, so the latter tend to fly into high-tension cables or fall prey to predators, because of their reduced alertness.

Grief also has a dramatic effect on goose social behavior. Grief-stricken geese are utterly unable to defend themselves from attacks launched by other geese. If a grieving goose has occupied an elevated position in the rigid hierarchy of the goose colony, its sudden defenselessness will be recognized and exploited with astounding speed by its former subordinates. It will be jostled and pushed from all sides, by even the weakest and least courageous members of the flock. In other words, it will sink to the lowest level in the pecking order, becoming, in the words of animal sociologists, the "omega animal."

As I said earlier, bereaved geese usually attempt to return to the family fold. It is incredibly touching when an old gander that was hand-reared many years ago but has shown no personal bond to its foster parent during a long and happy "marriage" abruptly returns to its human friend grief-stricken by the loss of its consort. Ado had been reared not by human foster parents but by his own mother, and she had died a long time ago. Also, he was not particularly tame. For example, he was not tame enough to take food out of our hands. That made it all the more touching when, after the death of Susanne-Elisabeth in the summer of 1976, he obstinately tried to attach himself to me, although he was less familiar with me than with Sybille Kalas or Brigitte Kirchmayer. It was some time before I noticed that whenever I moved away from the flock of greylag geese that were bullying poor Ado, following his fall in rank, he would shyly creep after me, his body hunched in sadness, and he would remain motionless about twenty-five or thirty feet away.

Ado spent the remainder of 1976 sad and isolated. Then, in the spring of 1977, he abruptly pulled himself together and began an intensive courtship of a goose called Selma. She was firmly paired off and had already reared three youngsters with her "husband," Gurnemanz, the previous year. Yet Ado's adoration was reciprocated by this unfaithful female, and there followed a highly unusual drama of jealousy.

Any "rightful" husband or bridegroom whose goose shows an interest in another gander has at his disposal several specific behavior patterns he can employ to prevent her from taking off with his rival. He can stick close to the female wherever she goes and bar her passage if she tries to move toward the other gander (21). If he is extremely provoked, he will even bite her—something he would never do under normal circumstances (22).

I can demonstrate such behavior right now with a male bean goose (*Anser fabalis* Linnaeus) that is jealous of me. Although his female companion, Camilla, is almost three years old, she displays a pronounced childish attachment to me. As soon as she sees me, she runs toward me and attempts to greet me. Despite this childish tendency, she became firmly betrothed to the male bean goose, Calvin, a year ago, and he is not pleased to see his "bride" give a friendly greeting to anyone else, even a human being. As a demonstration for visitors, I only need to call Camilla to me and elicit a greeting from her to provoke her suitor, Calvin, to display the entire range of jealous behavior described in the preceding paragraph.

A gander forced to guard his female in that manner is in a difficult and demanding position. He cannot leave his consort to attack his rival because the unfaithful female will break away the moment he leaves her side. He cannot feed properly, and if the drama lasts many weeks he eventually loses weight visibly. From dawn until late twilight one can see these goose "trios" moving across the landscape in a hurried procession. The rival favored by the female goose's attention is in front, followed by the goose herself, with the gander jealously maintaining his guard between them (23, 24, 25).

Fights between rival ganders become particularly intense when the goose herself is undecided about the object of her affection. The fiercest fights I can remember took place between two ganders, Blasius and Markus, in their competition for a goose called Alma. The two males were of equal strength, and Alma was obviously not sure which one she wanted for her mate.

I observed one aerial battle between the two ganders that could easily have taken a fatal course. Geese are well equipped for aerial combat: one will climb above the other in the sky, dive downward like a raptor, and swoop narrowly past to strike its opponent with a wing shoulder (the anatomical equivalent of our wrist). In this particular fight between the two brothers high in the air, Markus managed to strike Blasius with his wing shoulder at the root of the neck, directly in front of the wing. That is just where the nerve plexus that supplies the wing is located. Blasius dropped like a stone from a height of about sixty feet, his wing completely paralyzed. Luckily for him, he fell into the water. Had he fallen on rocks or on a hard gravel bed, he would undoubtedly have been killed. As it was, he suffered only a temporary paralysis; his wing hung limply for several days before recovering completely. Nonetheless, the incident demonstrates that fighting between rival ganders can easily have fatal results. I hardly need add that following his victory Markus walked off with the bride.

On level ground the fighting takes a different form. A greylag goose possesses two weapons: its beak, which can inflict a painful bite, and its wing shoulder, which is embellished with a small,

23

The drama of jealousy involving Selma, Gurnemanz, and Ado lasted almost two weeks. At first Gurnemanz attempted to drive Ado away in the air. Since Selma would follow her beloved Ado, however, wild aerial chases ensued, and the three geese often landed exhausted afterward, as in this picture taken in the Cumberland Foundation Wildlife Park. Gurnemanz can be seen blocking Selma's way once again. In the background, members of the goose flock follow events with great interest.

Once again, Gurnemanz bites Selma as a result of his great excitement. Ado, still somewhat uncertain about the situation, walks in the background with his neck tucked in.

25
That same evening, Gurnemanz is seen walking rapidly to and fro between Selma and Ado in an extremely "cowed" posture, in a desperate attempt to keep his female even after being defeated by his rival in a fight. Ado stands victorious in the background, adopting a demonstrative posture.

26

During a social upheaval such as that involved in the drama of jealousy just described, fighting with the wing shoulders—the geese's most extreme form of aggressive interaction—often occurs. Two rival ganders use their beaks to grasp each other by the feathers on the neck, breast, or flank. They pull them- *selves closer together by flexing their necks and then strike at each other with their wing shoulders, producing loud slapping noises audible some distance away. Other geese show an active interest in such incidents and follow the fighting closely, frequently gabbling as they do so.*

thornlike, thickly horn-covered bony projection, called the carpal spur. Fighting ganders grasp each other with their beaks, usually somewhere on the neck (26), and pull themselves close together, so that they are at just the right distance to administer blows with the wing shoulders. One wing is spread out wide behind as a counterbalance, and the other is bent at the wrist joint to position the horny weapon for flailing the opponent (27, 28). One can hear the smacking, slapping blows a long way off, and other ganders rush up excitedly to watch (29, 30).

Low-ranking geese are particularly eager to be spectators; geese high in the hierarchy, on the other hand, may sometimes join in the fight, but only if they are especially self-confident and courageous. They are most likely to join in when there has been the kind of jealous pursuit just described, since they are apparently agitated by the disruption this introduces into the flock.

The more usual fights, concerned with position in the social hierarchy, rarely escalate to the level of wing-shoulder duels; even when they do, they last only a few minutes. By contrast, a wing-shoulder fight between two ganders courting the same female can last more than a quarter of an hour and leave both opponents exhausted. Often, after an indecisive battle of this kind, the fight will resume the next day.

The most bitter fighting of all occurs in two quite specific social situations. The first of these situations involves two ganders who have previously been bound together by homosexual triumph calling. Their "love" suddenly turns to "hate," heralding an outbreak of fighting, and such hate can persist for years. Every time we have observed a persistent personal hatred between two ganders, a careful examination of our records has shown that they previously shared a homosexual bond.

The second situation leading to extremely bitter fighting has already been mentioned; it is when a goose is being courted by two ganders but is unable to decide firmly between them. In Selma's

27
In order to increase the striking range of their wings, fighting ganders hold their bodies as erect as possible and sometimes support themselves with their tail feathers.

47

28, 29, 30, 31
*Powerful blows with the wing shoulders
are exchanged until one of the opponents
gives up, turns away, and flees.*

case, her inclinations alternated a number of times between her "rightful husband," Gurnemanz, and her new suitor, Ado. That led to the dramatic fighting Sybille Kalas has recorded in her photographs.

The fights lasted for several days, until finally Gurnemanz gave up and fled, as his opponent tried to hold him firmly by the neck feathers (31). The victorious Ado then stood inflated with pride in a veritably eaglelike pose, his wings held so that the horny projections on the wing shoulders stood out as if he were brandishing brass knuckles (32).

After he had fled to a safe distance, Gurnemanz, the loser, sank to the ground completely exhausted (33). He was then attacked by the geese that had previously ranked below him in the social hierarchy. The poor gander, having lost his consort in the fights shown in the photographs, failed to defend himself against even the weakest opponents. Just like Ado two years previously, he had lost his social standing along with his wife.

The actual mating season comes soon after the period of great excitement surrounding pair formation and its resulting jealousies, but is quite distinctly separated from it. The individual pairs split away from the flock and begin to seek out nesting sites. In making their choices, different individuals frequently exhibit very different tastes and aptitudes. Most of our geese seek out nesting sites at the north end of Lake Alm, near its outlet, among marsh islands covered with reeds and rushes. Only a few of the geese breed in the fox-proof nest boxes we have constructed for them in the ponds at Oberganslbach. The lake is therefore the best place to observe the mating and brooding behavior of the geese, as can easily be seen in photograph 34.

The mating prelude begins when the gander adopts a proud posture somewhat resembling that of the mute swan. He lifts his wings and arches his neck in an elegant curve, while ruffling his neck feathers to such a degree that their grooves become clearly visible. In this posture, the gander dips his head deep into the water (35, 36).

56

32
If the stronger of two ganders succeeds in forcing his opponent to flee, he often adopts a long-lasting "victorious posture" and returns to his consort with a loud triumph call. This photo clearly shows the hard, horny spurs on the wing shoulders that are used in fighting.

33
After Ado had definitively appropriated Selma, Gurnemanz went to pieces, as can be seen in this picture. He sank to the ground in an extreme submissive posture as soon as he spotted his former rival. Geese adopt this posture as an expression of unconditional surrender in situations of extreme social stress or when physically exhausted.

Before the heavy spring runoff of water from the "Dead Mountain," Lake Alm falls to its lowest level. At this time, the geese spend a great deal of time on the exposed muddy banks on the southern shore of the lake. We often visit them there and spend many hours in their company. It is a good place to follow the formation of new pairs and the other social events that take place during the courtship period.

Mating between the geese always takes place in the water. Initially, the gander invariably adopts the so-called frigate posture, in which his neck is held in a proud S-shaped curve and both wings are slightly raised.

The goose responds by dipping her head in the same way, at first shyly and incompletely and then with gradually increasing excitation (37). She will then adopt a flat posture, exposing her neck to the gander. He grasps the goose's neck firmly in his beak (38), mounts her (39), and proceeds to copulate (40).

Copulation plays a comparatively small part in the cohesion of the greylag goose pair. Sometimes precocious young geese will mate in their first year, but that has no bearing on the future bonding of these individuals. If, on the other hand, one sees two immature geese performing the triumph-calling ceremony, one can predict with fair reliability that they will remain together in later life. Love and sex are two different things in the life of the goose. In combination, they help guarantee the healthy cohesion of the pair, but they can with some frequency occur independently. A typical case of such dissociation—one that is not uncommon—is when two ganders "fall in love with each other" to the extent that they perform the triumph-calling ceremony. They are not homosexual in the literal sense, since they never engage in sexual behavior together. It is anatomically possible for them to adopt the copulatory posture, but in fact copulation is rendered impossible because neither is prepared to assume the flat posture of the female described above and shown in photograph 38. Sometimes they will proceed to the stage of dipping their necks in the water, but then each male tries to mount the other and eventually they give up the copulation attempt, perhaps after some minor dispute. At any rate the close bond that exists between them is in no way disturbed by this "minor failure."

Understandably, these gander pairs are far superior to any normal pair in courage and fighting strength, since the gander is not only more courageous and aggressive than any female goose, but also heavier and stronger. Gander pairs always occupy a high rank in the social hierarchy of the goose colony. Accordingly, it is common for an unpaired female, impressed by the victories of the two heroes, to fall in love with one of them. As a rule, active courtship

*The next phase of the mating prelude
consists in neck dipping, in which the
gander dips his head into the water and
withdraws it, sending a shower of water
cascading over his head and neck.*

37
The goose in the foreground of this picture is similarly performing neck dipping.

*When the female is ready for mating,
she lies flat on the water and presents
her neck to the gander in such a way
that he can grasp it firmly in his beak
as he mounts her.*

The gander now mounts the goose.

40
When the gander has mounted the female, he twists his tail underneath hers on one side, presses his vent against hers, and protrudes his spirally coiled penis (characteristic of the duck and goose family). After copulation, the gander slides off the female's back, raises his neck, tail, and wings, and utters a typical mating call. Afterward, the two geese take a bath.

is conducted by the gander. The female goose behaves passively, and an infatuated female has no behavior patterns at her disposal to court the favors of her loved one; she lacks the techniques we have seen the gander use. All the female can do is stand around near the gander, as if by chance, and follow his behavior closely with her eyes. ("Eye play" apparently has an important role in the life of the greylag goose, as in that of other birds.)

Occasionally, after a gander pair has unsuccessfully attempted to copulate in the manner I have described above, an infatuated female goose will immediately swim up to the two males, adopt the flat posture, and as a result actually be mounted by one of them. The behavior can be repeated and may become habitual, leading to a highly unusual relationship. The two ganders continue to stay close together and are followed about inconspicuously by a single female, often some distance away. She does not participate in the triumph calling of the two males, but she is occasionally mounted by one of them. After copulation, however, the gander never performs toward her the magnificent ceremony of the post-mating display, an act that invariably follows a successful mating between a pair bonded by the triumph call and thus truly "in love."

In this regard, we once observed an extremely strange performance by a gander. Triumph-calling partnerships can involve three ganders, and in Seewiesen there were three such males—Max, Kopfschlitz, and Odysseus—that ruled over the entire goose colony on Lake Ess as a homosexual male triumvirate. Odysseus had developed with a female goose called Ona a "loveless copulatory relationship" of the kind just described. It was his habit to seek her out regularly at a certain spot some distance from the usual haunts of the triumvirate and copulate with her there. But as soon as the copulation was over, he would fly straight back across the lake to his two companions and perform toward them a fully accomplished postmating display, as if to say, "Actually, it was really meant for you."

An unloved mistress has only one way of gaining inclusion in the triumph-calling partnership of two ganders. First she must find a nest site and defend it against other nest-seeking geese (no easy matter, and rarely successful). Then she must be lucky enough to have her loved one see her brooding or, better still, accompanying her freshly hatched offspring. If that happens, the gander may adopt the goslings, defending and leading them. This behavior may also be exhibited by lonely ganders, particularly widowed ones. That is, they will adopt goslings not their own. With the adopted offspring—which, as we have seen, could be the gander's "illegitimate" heirs—the male will develop a proper family triumph-calling ceremony of the kind to be described shortly. The unloved mother of the accepted goslings may participate in this triumph calling and gradually be accepted as an equal member of the male partnership.

Among wild geese of various species one frequently finds trios, which typically consist of two males and a female. It is likely that they are always, or almost always, formed in the manner I have described. Such *ménages à trois* can therefore not be regarded as an abnormality, much less as some kind of pathological phenomenon. Peter Scott found them frequently among the pink-footed geese in Iceland and discovered that they were particularly successful in rearing offspring, since defense of the family by two dashing ganders was far more efficient than by one alone.

A dissociation of love and copulation can occur with other geese besides those joined by a homosexual bond. In pairs that have developed a firm triumph-calling bond at an early stage and are well adapted in other respects, the male is usually—and the female always—absolutely monogamous and faithful, even in the strictest sexual sense. But if the love bond is not quite so pronounced, as, for example, when the gander has lost his first love and has paired off with another female, that is a different matter. The male will defend his rightful consort with courage and fidelity, helping her choose a nest site, carrying out his nest-watching duties correctly, and participating diligently in the guidance and defense of his offspring. Despite his very proper behavior toward his family, however, he is ready to mount any strange female that proffers an invitation. Yet he will pay no further attention to the passing female, failing to defend her and not responding even if she is seized and carried off before his very eyes, as I was able to determine experimentally on one occasion. In a similar situation, he would defend his "legitimate" consort at the risk of his life.

Interestingly, this kind of dissociation between love and copulation is found much more frequently in male geese than in females. All the "unloved" females that were incorporated into partnerships in the cases I have just cited were demonstrably "in love" with the ganders with whom they were willing to copulate. In more objective terms, they were always ready to join in triumph calling with the male if he exhibited the slightest inclination in that direction.

Unlike pregnancy in mammals, pregnancy in birds—including geese—begins somewhat before the sexual act itself. In fish, pregnancy in fact terminates with mating; the sperm and the eggs are discharged at the same time. In birds, the eggs are fertilized within the mother's body when the yolks are already quite large, and a female goose's belly will begin to swell noticeably even before the mating season has reached its peak (41).

The pair will then begin to search actively for a nest site. Sometimes they show great skill at this, but sometimes they are downright careless. Some pairs seek out a well-concealed nest site, as was true of the female pictured (42), which had successfully bred at the same spot twice previously. Some geese nest in relatively exposed areas on islands. The water provides limited protection against foxes, but the lack of cover over the nest makes it accessible to crows and ravens, which, unfortunately, are especially partial to goose eggs. Other geese prefer isolated and somewhat elevated nest sites, as was the case with Selma, the female whose drama of jealousy we have recounted (43). Unhappily, geese are just as inclined to nest on peninsulas as on real islands; they are apparently unable to understand that these nests are fully exposed to foxes. Under natural conditions, nesting geese typically choose a spot that is hidden behind sparse cover of some kind but at the same time has

41
In early spring, during the courtship period, the eggs begin to mature in the female's abdomen and the yolk forms. Soon the female has the characteristic swollen belly indicating that she is ready to lay. The goose Hexe, shown in this picture, has a bald patch on her neck where the gander has pulled out a few feathers every time he has mounted her.

42
Some geese prefer nesting sites on small islands in the delta of Lake Alm that are covered with low vegetation suitable for grazing. This rather shy goose remains quite calm as we approach her nest, though she keeps a watchful eye on us.

74

an unhindered view in all directions. Thus they can see without being seen. Surprisingly, however, they are also more or less willing to occupy nest boxes closed on all sides, except for a small entrance, so long as the boxes are erected on poles in the middle of a body of water. Since we of course want to be sure that our geese breed successfully, we will correct an obviously careless choice of a nest site by removing the offending goose's eggs, in the hope that she will lay a second clutch in a more suitable place, where she can breed undisturbed.

The story surrounding the successful breeding of one goose is perhaps of interest here. Sybille Kalas had devoted special attention to a goose called Alma, which she had hand-reared in 1974, in order to keep the goose as tame as possible. When I am asked what kind of care that involves, I reply, "Roughly the same as you would devote to a young dog in order to bring it up as a friendly and loyal companion. You must take the dog out for walks as often as possible, spend a lot of time talking to it, and if possible allow it to sleep in the same room with you."

The same bonding principles are applicable with geese. The more one wanders around with them, and the farther away one takes them, the more attached they become. It is likewise effective to share one's nest with them. That is why our goose keepers are expected to sleep with their geese; the huts at Oberganslbach were designed with this purpose in mind. The fact that under certain conditions it can lead to considerable discomfort is shown by photograph 104, on page 149.

Sybille Kalas meticulously fulfilled all these duties with Alma and her siblings, with the result that Alma was still extraordinarily attached to her when the goose bred for the first time, in the spring of 1976.

The scientific goal of the considerable investment of work and time was to produce a goose family whose parents were completely tame, so that all the family interaction between them and their offspring could be observed and investigated at close quarters in minute

76

detail. Such a family was essential to our studies of social behavior because it was important for us to know whether and to what degree young geese who had been reared by us behaved differently toward us than naturally reared geese behaved toward their real parents.

It was a lucky coincidence that Alma paired off with a gander of the same age, hand-reared by Brigitte Kirchmayer. It was, in fact, the same Markus whose bitter struggles with the gander Blasius I have recounted. All the effort Sybille had expended in raising Alma would have been wasted if she had paired off with a shy gander reared by his own parents. Such a male would have undermined Alma's relationship with Sybille through jealous behavior like that described on page 40. Markus, however, was extremely friendly with humans, and we were pleased when the two geese selected for breeding a nest box that had been set up on poles in a pond at Oberganslbach, not far from the hut in which Sybille lived. Alma had just laid her first egg when, to our considerable annoyance, she was driven away from her nest by a pair of brent geese. They in turn were soon chased off by another pair of greylag geese, which had designs on the same nest box. All this happened on April 11, 1976, a day when the temperature was hovering around freezing and deep snow had fallen. As chance would have it, Sybille did not have with her a pair of the chest-high wading trousers that fishermen wear, which we use when constructing nest boxes in the ponds. But fast action was required, and Sybille, who was alone in Oberganslbach, heroically went out to the defense of Alma's nest. She undressed and waded through the ice-cold water to chase off the intruding geese. Imagine the scene: barely daybreak, thirty-two degrees Fahrenheit, a thick snowstorm, and water at least five feet deep.

The wicked interlopers were driven off, but the damage had been done. Alma did not return to that nest. Instead, she constructed an emergency nest several hundred yards upstream from Oberganslbach, which contained three eggs by the time we found it. The nest lay on dry land in a fairly exposed spot on the bank of the

river Alm, and it would certainly have been found by either foxes or ravens—or by both at once. So Sybille removed the eggs and placed them in the original nest box, in which Alma's first egg was still sitting. To Sybille's great pleasure, Alma then laid a fifth egg in the nest box. But satisfaction soon turned to annoyance when Alma was again chased away by the wicked brent geese. That this could happen was largely attributable to the fact that Markus, for all his tameness and friendship for humans, was an out-and-out coward in his contacts with other geese. He proved to be somewhat lacking in the brood-care drive, as was confirmed later by his behavior during the rearing of the offspring.

After that, we all thought Alma would not succeed in breeding that summer, yet ten days later she had started to build a new nest, on an island in Lake Alm. Here she laid and incubated her eggs. Since we attached particular importance to that clutch, we visited the nest daily and discovered that Alma would greet Sybille in complete friendship. Showing no resistance at all, she would permit Sybille to remove the eggs one at a time and hold them up to the light or smell them! A rotten egg can explode in a nest, and the decaying egg white that is scattered around will clog the pores of the other eggs, causing the embryos to suffocate. Photograph 44 shows how Sybille fed Alma with one hand while sniffing underneath her to see whether any of the eggs had begun to decay.

During brooding pauses, Alma continued to seek out Sybille and keep her company, encountering no objection from the tame but spiritless Markus. Brooding pauses are an essential part of the goose's brooding behavior. The eggs must cool so that the air in the egg cavity will contract and fresh air will be sucked in through the pores of the eggshell. Even with goose eggs that are artificially incubated, regular brooding pauses must be replicated. During each brooding pause, the goose not only drinks and grazes, but also bathes, so that the eggs will be moistened on her return.

Before the goose leaves her nest to take a brooding pause, she carefully covers the eggs with the down feathers that line the nest and form a sort of rampart around it. At the beginning of incubation she has pulled these feathers from her own belly and pushed

44
Alma is so tame that Sybille Kalas can check her eggs without forcing her to get up from the nest. By sniffing the eggs, one can quickly tell whether there is a bad one in the nest. While the nest is being checked, Alma eats from her former foster mother's hand.

45
Although Alma knows me, she attacks me with bites and wing-shoulder blows to drive me away from her nest. Only a few minutes earlier she had allowed her foster mother, Sybille, to feed her.

46
Several times a day, the goose turns over the eggs in the nest by tucking her beak under them and pulling them toward her. Eggs that have fallen out of the nest are rolled back with the same movement. By regularly turning the eggs, the goose prevents the membrane from adhering firmly to the shell.

47

During the brooding season, we visit the tame geese on their nests every day, and from time to time we give them food as well. If they can spend the intervals between brooding spells in our company they are particularly content. When the goslings eventually hatch, the mothers have grown so used to our presence that we can observe each family at close quarters without difficulty.

them between and beneath the eggs. The primary function of the down feathers during the brooding pause is not to serve as a heat-insulating layer, since the eggs must cool, but, rather, as camouflage, to protect them from the watchful eyes of ravens and crows. The brooding pause can last from ten minutes to more than an hour. When the goose returns to the nest, she will usually stand over the eggs for a while, carefully cleaning the plumage on her belly, before she turns the eggs by tucking her beak over each one and rolling it toward her (46). Very tame geese can be fed while on the nest, and we take advantage of that to divert their attention when we want to check the eggs (47).

Covering the eggs with down feathers and nest material protects them from crows and ravens, which seek out their prey by sight, but not from predatory mammals that rely on smell for orientation. The beautiful raven, which has become rare in other places, is still frequently found in the Alm Valley, and ravens are particularly abundant within the wildlife park, where they are attracted by the food set out for bears, wolves, and other predators. Old ravens have a wonderful technique for stealing half-gnawed bones from the wolf enclosure when none of those predators is looking; younger, less experienced birds often pay for such impertinence with their lives. The raven is a magnificent bird, but we hate to see one perching in a tree near a goose nest (48), since we are likely to find the nest later in the condition shown in photograph 49. Geese are well aware that ravens and crows represent a threat to their nests, but we do not know whether this is an innate property or whether they have learned it from unfortunate experience. We have often seen brooding geese attack crows or ravens on the wing, when the geese have spotted their enemy perched in an exposed position high in the trees above the nests. It was a new experience for me to see a raven taking such an attack seriously—though not surprising, when one considers how effective a blow delivered by a greylag goose's wing shoulder can be.

The goslings hatch after about a month of incubation. The gander also takes up a position by the nest then (50). We have been

48

When the geese begin to lay, ravens and crows soon appear near the nests, awaiting a suitable opportunity to steal eggs from unguarded nests. We have often observed ganders, while keeping watch in their brooding territories, take off to attack crows in the air and drive them off.

49

Despite the vigilance of the geese, ravens and crows now and then succeed in stealing and eating eggs. The broken shells can often be found near the nests.

unable to figure out how he knows when the right time has come. It is definitely not due to any "internal clock," since the gander takes his position just before hatching even if the original eggs have been exchanged for a clutch that will hatch considerably earlier. In all likelihood, he is alerted to the imminent hatching of the goslings by their vocalizations from within the egg. He may notice them directly, while in the vicinity of the nest, or indirectly, by some signal from the mother after she has heard peeping calls from within the eggs. In fact, the mother begins to communicate with her offspring sometime before they hatch from the egg. She utters faint contact calls to the goslings in their eggs, and the latter are capable of producing a number of different calls, which indicate to the mother whether they are developing normally. When the offspring produce a plaintive call, known as "lost piping," the mother responds with contact calls as if to comfort them, to which the unborn goslings sometimes respond in their turn with greeting calls. When a gosling begins to pipe from an intact egg, the mother often reacts by turning the egg over. After the goslings have hatched or are in the process of hatching, the goose will raise herself slightly, lift her wings (51), and look down at her offspring. She pays special attention to the empty eggshells, which must quickly be removed from the nest, since they can be dangerous to the hatching offspring. But mistakes sometimes occur. We once saw a goose throw into the water an eggshell from which the gosling had only half emerged.

During the first few days after hatching, the goslings become increasingly restless, emerging more and more frequently from beneath the mother and making small excursions nearby (53). Then the great moment arrives when the mother rises from the nest and slowly leaves it, all the while uttering contact calls. The goslings follow her in a tight-packed formation (52).

In their first few days of life the goslings must frequently be warmed, roughly every fifteen to twenty minutes. While this is happening they will often thrust their heads out through the mother's feathers and direct toward her face a greeting cackle, indicating their family bond (54). If the mother gets up and moves off, the goslings follow closely behind (55).

50
When the goslings are ready for hatching and begin to utter calls from inside the eggs, the gander comes to join the female, instead of keeping watch some distance from the nest. In this picture, Ado is hissing at us in threat as we approach his female, Selma, on her nest.

51
Very tame geese, such as Cressida in this photo, allow us to visit the nest to examine the freshly hatched goslings. These two goslings have been hatched for about half an hour. The down feathers are still covered with their sheaths, which will soon drop away as a fine dust. The gosling on the left has already begun to fixate his mother with one eye, and she is returning his gaze, while the gosling on the right nibbles at some dry grass at the edge of the nest. Both these behavior patterns are vitally important to the small goslings. The first is necessary for recognition of the mother; the other is needed for learning the difference between edible and inedible objects.

52
This family has just left the nest. Under the leadership of the gander, now standing watchfully by his consort and their offspring, the group has swum to the bank of the creek surrounding their brooding island. The mother at once sinks to the ground so that the goslings can creep beneath her. But the goslings are not tired yet and spend some time nibbling inquisitively at the dry grass on the bank.

53

The goslings remain beneath their mother on the nest for the first day after hatching. Then they begin to make small excursions and in this way gradually prepare themselves for the definitive departure from the nest. The two goslings in this picture are avidly pecking and nibbling at grass stems and small sticks, though they are not actually eating anything.

54

When the small goslings are cold or tired, they burrow beneath their mother's feathers with oblique upward thrusts of their heads. As a result, they often re-emerge higher up, as is the case here. When the gosling spots its mother, it directs a greeting call toward her head.

55
*Tight family cohesion is vitally impor-
tant for the goslings. As soon as the
mother starts moving, they follow her
closely on foot.*

55
Tight family cohesion is vitally important for the goslings. As soon as the mother starts moving, they follow her closely on foot.

56

During their first days of life, the goslings learn which food plants are palatable and which are relatively unpalatable. They do so partly by nibbling at a wide variety of plants and partly by observing exactly what their parents eat.

57
The rare buckbean (Menyanthes tri-foliata L.) *blooms in May on the swampy islands and promontories of Lake Alm.*

58
In the same spots and at the same time of year one can also find cotton sedge (Eriophorum L.).

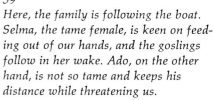

59
Here, the family is following the boat. Selma, the tame female, is keen on feeding out of our hands, and the goslings follow in her wake. Ado, on the other hand, is not so tame and keeps his distance while threatening us.

Laymen often have erroneous ideas about what the parents of different animal species teach their offspring. It is said that swallows have to teach their infants to fly and other such nonsense. Most of the patterns of movement required for survival are innate in virtually all bird species, especially those with immediately mobile offspring, like the greylag goose. The movements made by the small gosling in pecking and swallowing edible items are completely innate, though the gosling must learn *what* is edible. There, the drive to imitate the parents plays an important part. In the first few days after hatching, the goslings watch closely what the parents are eating and then peck at the same objects (56). We were able to observe clearly the influence of parental example during the year when Alma was leading her first offspring. As a hand-reared goose, Alma was quite familiar with the food we used and ate it greedily whenever it was offered. Meanwhile, a timid greylag goose that had been reared by her natural parents was leading her young on Lake Alm. She was unable to find much in the way of food in the peat moss there, and we would have liked to offer her some of our nourishing gosling food. But she would not accept it because her own parents were not familiar with it and refused to touch it. At the time the tiny goslings are leaving the nest, the marshy islands where the geese forage are bedecked with the flowers of buckbean (*Menyanthes trifoliata* Linnaeus, 57) and cotton sedge (*Eriophorum* Linnaeus, 58).

It is only a few days before the diminutive goslings are able to walk and, even more so, to swim unbelievable distances (59, 60, 61), covering several miles in the company of their parents. For example, they could travel the three and a half miles from Lake Alm to our observation area, as shown in photograph 1 and others. Oddly enough, both the old and the young geese seem to be afflicted by a pronounced wanderlust within a few days after the hatching. Goose families that have bred on Lake Alm suddenly arrive at Oberganslbach, and there are also arrivals from downstream, where some of the geese have bred on the large pond in the wildlife park. The goose pair Lukas and Hexe marched out of the park in fairly deep snow one year with five goslings and arrived at Oberganslbach with only

three remaining. It is a reasonable assumption that all the movement is motivated by an urge to return to Oberganslbach, where many of the geese grew up. Only a single pair that had bred in Oberganslbach moved off to Lake Alm with its young, and neither of those parents had grown up in Oberganslbach.

Sybille Kalas undertook a careful study of the local migration from Lake Alm to Oberganslbach, which some pairs of geese make regularly every year. She was spurred to do the study not only because the migration is dangerous and often leads to the loss of some goslings, but also because that aspect of goose behavior has great inherent interest. The geese generally set off early in the morning, although sometimes they do not leave until late afternoon. That was the case with Selma, her new offspring, and her husband, Ado, in 1977. Selma had been hand-reared by Sybille a year before Alma and was almost as firmly attached to her. Sybille knew that the geese were on the move and went out to meet them. She found them on an island in the middle of a fast-flowing stretch of water that they were afraid to enter. For two hours she patiently tried to lure them across, without success. The geese repeatedly approached the water's edge, tried to enter, and turned back. Then, without further ado, Sybille caught the three goslings, carried them across the river, and released them on the bank. The parents immediately followed, and now they decided to lead their offspring toward Oberganslbach along a road bearing heavy traffic. Sybille headed them off and drove them back to the river, where the family promptly took to the water and began swimming sedately and purposefully downstream in the direction of Oberganslbach. But the river Alm flows much faster than even the long-legged Sybille can run, and the geese were soon way out in front. At that point Selma uttered separation calls, and the geese stopped to wait for Sybille to catch up with them. Then they had to be prevented once more from moving over to what seemed to them like the more convenient road. The road did indeed lead directly to Oberganslbach and certainly appeared to be more convenient—except that the geese were unable to appreciate its dangers. Eventually they went through the wood, not once losing their way along a path that only the mother had taken previously, as a young goose and traveling in the opposite direction. The entire convoy at last reached Oberganslbach in late twilight. Ado and Selma first took a bath in relief, then had supper in Sybille's hut, and finally went off to sleep in the security of the island. Unfortunately, we have no photographic record of that magnificent journey Sybille took with the wild geese. However, since she had to wade across the Alm several times, in rushing water that was well above her waist, it was probably just as well she did not have her valuable camera with her.

At a very early age the siblings hatched by a particular pair begin to develop a social hierarchy. Typically, their first fights occur early in the morning, sometimes before daybreak, and these therefore escaped our attention until Sybille Kalas noticed them in 1971. The tiny goslings quite abruptly start fighting vigorously, in a sort of general free-for-all.

The response of the parents, which are obviously somewhat disturbed by the situation, is remarkable. They stare tensely and excitedly at the fighting goslings, often spreading their wings and hissing. The effect is as if a small predator had infiltrated the group of goslings but had then become invisible (62). However, the parents never intervene to stop the fighting among the goslings, except that the mother will offer protection to any defeated goslings that flee from the fight and attempt to bury themselves beneath her.

In their fights the tiny goslings display exactly the same fighting behavior as adult geese. They can bite just as effectively as adults, and pull in the same way at an opponent's feathers (63). They also attempt to strike each other with their wing shoulders, just as adult ganders do, but that comes to nothing because their wings are still too short. A gosling will grasp its opponent with its beak and maintain a distance that would bring the opponent within range of the carpal spur if the body proportions were the same as in an adult goose. The gosling will also bend its wing at the wrist joint the same as an adult does, but the wing is so short that the gosling succeeds only in striking its own flank. The other wing is held straight backward as a counterbalance, again like the adult's (64).

In their first days of life the goslings are involved in rank-order fights. The parents watch the process with interest, but never intervene.

63
The fighting goslings grasp each other by the neck feathers and attempt to strike each other with their wing shoulders, just as adult geese do.

The gosling on the right is just about to hit out with its wing shoulder, but it cannot reach its sibling because its wings are still far too short.

65
Alma's goslings are already fourteen
days old in this photo, and the space
available between the mother's wings is
becoming somewhat overstretched.

*During the midday heat the goslings like
to lie in the shadows cast by their
parents.*

The offspring are warmed by the mother as long as they remain small enough to find room under her wings (65). When they want to be warmed, they produce a faint trilling call, the sleeping call, and crowd up to the mother from behind. Similarly, if they become too hot in strong sunshine they will lie down in the parents' shadow, provided that the latter stand still long enough. In fact, usually they do, but we do not know whether they are deliberately cooling the goslings in this way (66). The only bird that is definitely known to cool its infants on purpose is the white stork.

This is perhaps the place to say a few words about the way goose parents lead their offspring. In the very first days after hatching it is almost entirely the parents' decision when to move off and in what direction—though the emphasis is on the "almost"! As the goslings grow older, they increasingly tend to behave independently, and never more so than when they are too hot. Particularly when their down feathers are being replaced and the goslings are, in a sense, carrying double plumage, they easily become overheated, even though the temperature may be perfectly acceptable to the parents. The goslings will head energetically for shade, obliging the parents to follow them by uttering persistent plaintive calls. As they grow older, the influence of the offspring on the overall behavior of the goose flock increases. We are especially interested in the influences that the parents still exert over their young at later stages.

The touchingly pretty appearance of the very young goslings (67) changes in the course of four or five days, producing quite a different impression, as is shown in the photograph of a four-day-old gosling (68).

The behavior of the goslings changes just as rapidly as their appearance. It is a continuing source of surprise to see how soon a pretty little ball of fluff turns into a majestic bird flying high in the sky. The development of behavior in the individual and, more important, in the structure of the goose family as a whole, along with the patterns of communication involved, is of special significance to our studies. Because our goose parents lead their offspring back to the site of their own infancy and bring them up before our eyes, alongside human foster parents with their adopted goslings,

67
Very young greylag goslings look rounded and fluffy, just like willow catkins.

68
At the age of four days the goslings have already developed the typical "goose face."

106

we are in a good position to make comparisons and to find out where we may be going wrong in our goose-rearing program. One of my young co-workers, Colombe Smith, once said to me in all seriousness, "I still have a lot to learn—from Hexe." Hexe, you will remember, is the goose that marched her goslings through deep snow from the wildlife park back to Oberganslbach.

Oberganslbach has been depicted in photograph 2 at the beginning of this book, and I have mentioned that the young scientists who work there live in delightful little huts designed by Herr Hüthmayer and constructed alongside our ponds (73).

The goose families that move in from Lake Alm eat at the same feeding troughs as the hand-reared geese (74, 75). We are in the midst of the most enchanting vegetation. Around the huts bloom barberries (*Berberis vulgaris* Linnaeus, 69), gentians (*Gentiana clusii* Linnaeus, 70), lady's slipper (*Cypripedium calceolus* Linnaeus, 71)—which has become quite rare elsewhere—and narcissus (*Narcissus poeticus* Linnaeus, 72). The narcissus are especially prevalent on the goose meadows because the geese do not touch their leaves while keeping the surrounding grasses short.

Every year a remarkable social life develops between the geese and the goose watchers at this beautiful haven. Goose families, in particular those united by blood relationships or by friendship, bring their infants together in a kind of play school. Of course, the groups of goslings do not become inextricably mixed, and an infant in need of warmth will not seek shelter beneath any goose except its mother. But the families maintain a close contact, so that if danger threatens, an interesting form of communal defense is possible. If a predatory bird dives down upon the geese, the goslings from all the families immediately rush to form a compact cluster while every parent spreads its wings and joins in a defensive circle around them. The excited calling and hissing of the united parents is quite capable of frightening off a large predator. We have set off this response by sending a stuffed goshawk sliding on rollers along a taut wire above the geese. We have a fine film of that experiment, but unfortunately no still photographs are available to illustrate it here.

108

70, 71, 72
Close to the huts in Oberganslbach can be found the flowers of gentian (Gentiana clusii L.), lady's slipper (Cypripedium calceolus L.), and narcissus (Narcissus poeticus L.).

73
Sybille Kalas at the entrance of her goose hut in Oberganslbach. The scientists who work with the geese, as well as their assistants, live in this hut and two others like it from March to September. This provides the opportunity not only for rearing the young geese undisturbed but also for observing the behavior of the other geese in the Grünau flock.

70, 71, 72
Close to the huts in Oberganslbach can be found the flowers of gentian (Gentiana clusii L.), lady's slipper (Cypripedium calceolus L.), and narcissus (Narcissus poeticus L.).

109

Alma and Markus arrive at the hut with their three offspring, Flicka, Astro, and Aurel, to feed without fear. The parents have already shed their primary feathers, while the offspring are just beginning to sprout their tail feathers and wing coverts.

When the family is being fed from a
small dish, the parents stand back to let
their offspring eat first.

Alma's infants are already five weeks
old. Their plumage is almost complete,
with the exception of the primaries. On
the neck and back of the head they still
bear the yellow down feathers that can
create a commical "coiffure" on geese of
this age.

77
*When the goslings are asleep, Alma pre-
fers to go to an elevated spot to keep
watch. In this picture, she is seen hissing
in threat toward a strange goose family.*

78
*While Alma and her offspring are preen-
ing themselves, Markus tensely keeps
watch in the direction of the forest.*

Goose fathers that have been hand-reared by human foster
parents, and to a lesser degree a small number of other ganders that
are relatively tame, tend to attach themselves to human keepers who
are leading young goslings, in the same way as any ganders seek
out the company of other ganders leading infants. A truly idyllic
relationship can develop (76). The young scientists leading their
geese try to behave as much like geese as they can, and it is a striking and highly satisfying sight to observe the leisurely progress of a
flock consisting of inextricably intermingled geese and young
people.

When the young geese are a few weeks old, their downy feathers are replaced by their definitive plumage. The feathers grow from
the same roots as the down, and for a while down can be seen hanging from the tips of the growing feathers, before it eventually
falls off. The down remains longest on the back of the head and the
upper part of the neck.

After the goslings have grown big enough for them no longer
to need to be warmed under the mother's wings, the parents lose
their primary feathers (79). Healthy geese shed all their primaries
almost simultaneously. Mostly this happens when the geese beat
their wings or preen themselves. But the resulting inability to fly
does not prevent the father of the goose family from performing
his role as lookout and guardian. The gander shown (78) tensely
keeping an eye on the wood—Markus, Alma's mate—has lost his
primaries. Barely a week after the loss of the primary feathers, the
new feathers have grown considerably, as can be seen when a goose
preens itself (80). It takes three to four weeks more before the
parents can fly again, by which time the primary feathers will have
grown another inch or so. That corresponds neatly with the period
during which the young geese are fledging—a beautiful example of
natural adaptation.

It also heralds a somewhat dangerous time for the young geese.
In a strict sense, they do not have to learn to fly, since the motor
coordination patterns required for takeoff, level flight, braking, and
landing are completely innate. However, they do have to learn how

115

79
*Once a year, in June, the geese lose all
their primary feathers and are unable to
fly until the replacement feathers have
grown, some four weeks later. A healthy
goose will lose all its primaries within
a short space of time, while preening or
shaking itself.*

80
*In the course of preening herself, Alma
has withdrawn one wing from the flank
feathers. Clearly visible are the blue
vascular sheaths, which have already
split at their ends to expose the tips of
the new primaries. Alma will be able
to fly again in three to four weeks' time.*

to estimate distances, differences in height, and, especially, wind conditions. Young geese have to learn that they can land only against the wind, and that they may turn the most awful somersaults if they land with the wind. A human foster parent can help with this to some extent by inducing them to land when they happen to fly in low against the wind. If the foster parent stoops rapidly, or falls flat on the ground, the young geese will respond in the same way as they do to a landing made by a parental guide—they will land at any cost. Understandably, the moment of the parents' landing is critical because of the danger that young geese afraid to land will lose contact with their guiding parents. I have carried out the somewhat brutal experiment of inducing young geese, in the manner just described, to land with the wind, something that inevitably leads to a "crash landing." The four young geese I was leading at the time were undamaged by the experiment, but it was obvious they had lost confidence in me! For some time afterward I was unable to induce them to land by abruptly dropping to the ground.

Sybille Kalas observed one interesting effect of parental guidance on young geese that have just fledged. When the youngsters want to take off on the wing and communicate this intention to their parents by spreading their wings and shaking their beaks, the parents utter warning calls and inhibit them from flying away. We know from our contact with hand-reared geese that the young birds are able to fly much earlier than they actually do—even before the primary feathers have grown long enough for the tips to cross over when the wings are folded. They will often fly off independently, and unfortunately accidents are far from rare. On one occasion, a young goose flew into the wall of a house at the height of three feet. We could see on the wall the traces made by the legs swung forward in the braking position. The corpse of the goose lay right underneath; death was due to a ruptured liver.

Such accidents are generally avoided through the warning, inhibitory influence of the parents. They are much less common with family-raised young geese than with those that are hand-reared. But the parents have another way of averting aerial acci-

When a goose removes the primaries
from their pockets, the elegant sickle-
shaped bastard wing is exposed to view.

*This hand-reared goose, Sinda, one of
Alma's sisters, displays the beauty of her
freshly completed juvenile plumage.*

dents. When, despite parental attempts to inhibit them, young geese
fly off, the parents take off after them, assume the lead at once, and
thus determine the landing site. Since the parents' wings are still
relatively short, they fly carefully, avoiding sharp turns and flashy
braking maneuvers. Without the offspring's being aware of it, the
parents are giving them valuable guidance. Above all, the parents
show the young geese what are good sites for landing and how to
make safe landings. One can see in photograph 77 that the mother
displaying threat toward another goose family has short new
primary feathers.

A goose's plumage is never again as handsome as it is immediately after fledging (82). All the feathers are equally new then, the
only time that happens in the bird's entire life. Most beautiful are
the feathers of the so-called bastard wing, or alula, which serve a
function comparable to that of the landing flaps of an airplane (81),
especially in takeoff and braking. The tips of the finished contour
feathers at first still bear the down feathers that formed the plumage
of the freshly hatched gosling (83). Once the down has fallen away,
the plumage has an appearance of unblemished smoothness, as can
be seen in photograph 84.

Besides the plumage, another feature of the goose that should
be noted is the feet. The scales that cover them are an age-old
inheritance from the reptilian stock that gave rise to the birds'
ancestors (85, 86). Rings are attached to the feet of the geese as
markers. The aluminum ring is from the bird station at Radolfzell,
on Lake Constance, which is devoted to avian migratory research.
A record of the ring numbers is maintained at Radolfzell, and we
receive word from there if any of our geese are sighted in far-off
places. If the goose is still alive, we will go to great expense to have
it brought back unharmed. Colored plastic rings allow us to identify
each goose individually, according to our own code; a ring above
the aluminum tag indicates the year of birth.

The great persistence of family bonds among greylag geese
makes them a particularly suitable subject for behavioral research,

83

The first down feathers are still present on the tips of the contour feathers, since one papilla gives rise to both and the down feathers are, so to speak, pushed along as their successors develop.

84

When the last down feathers have dropped away, the juvenile plumage has a perfectly smooth appearance. Never again during its lifetime will a goose have such a uniform plumage, since from now on the different types of feathers will form at different times. Molting of the secondaries occurs after that of the primaries, toward the end of June.

85, 86
All our geese carry numbered identifica-
tion rings issued by the bird observatory
at Radolfzell, along with a combination
of colored plastic rings indicating the
year of birth, the method of rearing,
and family relationships.

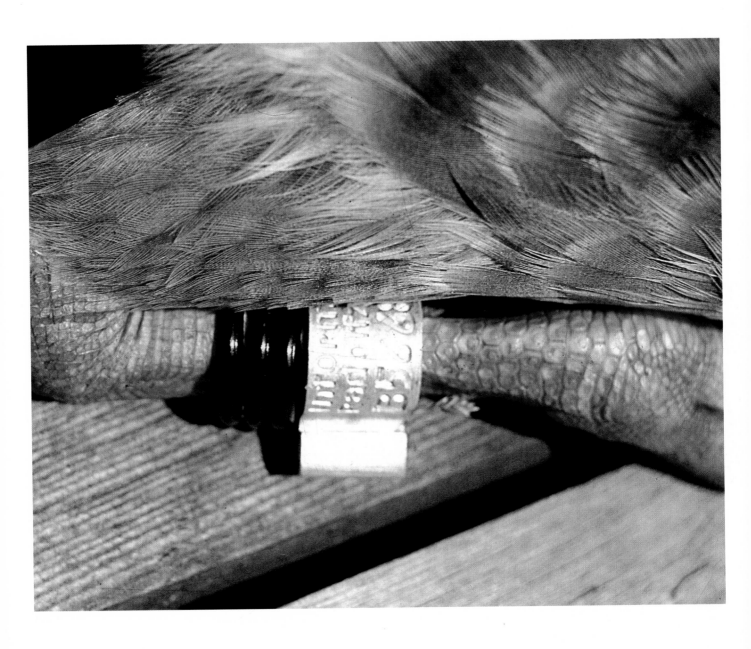

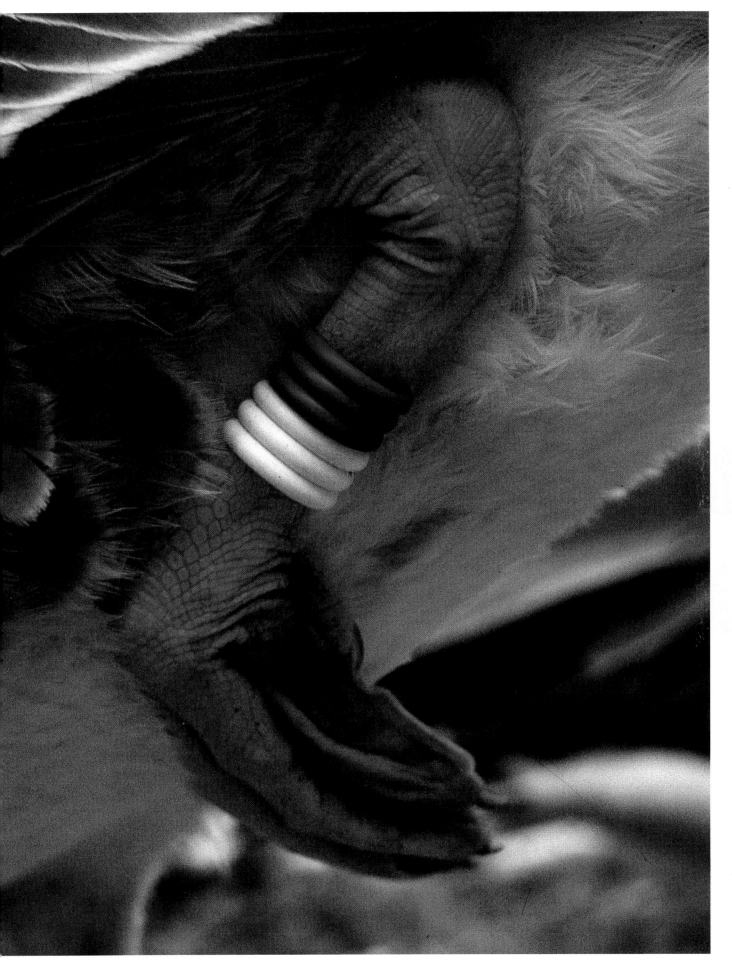

87
The older the offspring become, the less does an individual family maintain its distance from other geese. When the nonbreeding geese return from molting on Lake Alm, the goslings learn the position occupied by their family in the general ranking and soon join their parents in directing threat displays at other geese.

especially in the field of animal sociology. In most duck species, the offspring maintain no obvious relationship with their parents after fledging; young geese, however, retain very close family ties and will, for instance, take an active part in a dispute between their parents and other goose families (87). The gander in the photograph, barely seven weeks old—one of the famous Alma's sons—can be seen spearheading a family attack on some opponents. A familiarity with the molting process described earlier allows one to calculate the relative youth of the little hero, both from his own juvenile plumage and from the shortness of the parents' wing tips, which are not fully grown. It is from their participation in disputes involving the family that young geese come to recognize the rank their parents occupy in the goose flock. The youngsters automatically adopt the same rank, and it is amusing to see a half-grown goose cheekily approach a full-grown gander and, for example, drive him away from the food dish. However, that can be carried off successfully only if the family—and particularly the youngster's father—is not far away. I have observed the offspring of high-ranking families take a terrible beating from lower-ranking geese when caught well away from their families.

As soon as the young geese have attained full flying capacity, the molting of the secondaries begins—somewhat earlier in old geese than in young ones. Photograph 88 shows a goose with two offspring fully ready for flying. In the mother one can see the onset of the molt of the secondaries; the dark new feathers are clearly visible.

Once the youngsters are fully equipped for flight, the parents begin to take them on more ambitious excursions into the surrounding countryside. Frequently, several families will join for these excursions. In photograph 89, a group of families can be seen flying away from our pond in the direction of Lake Alm. In their first major flights, the geese often return to the pond (91), rather than landing at a distant spot. These flights take place at the time when the ragged robin (*Lychnis flos-cuculi* Linnaeus, 90) is in flower.

It is heartening when the time for learning to fly passes with-

After bathing (usually during the midday period), the geese preen themselves extensively, particularly during the molt, which is obvious in this picture from the many feathers lying on the ground. This is the way they remove the horny sheaths lining the new feathers.

When the young geese return from their practice flights, they often encounter difficulty in swooping upward from the river to clear the trees on the banks and then diving sharply down to land. In gliding down, the inexperienced geese often lose their balance and veer from one side to the other. Their struggle to keep on an even keel is accompanied by pitiful distress calls.

89

The young geese take their first excursions away from Oberganslbach by flying up and down the river Alm. When they are covering only short distances, however, they do not take up the usual V formation.

90

The pink-red flowers of the ragged robin (Lychnis flos-cuculi L.) are a typical sight on the meadows in the summer.

out loss. Again and again, one is amazed to see how in four short weeks the fluid content of an egg can bring forth a downy gosling that will cry and make greetings, grieve and be happy, and is capable of attaching itself to one certain individual—either a greylag goose or a human being. And every year it is a renewed source of wonderment how in eight more weeks the pretty little balls of fluff have changed into full-grown wild geese that fly way up into the sky in orderly formations and brave the storm.

Now, suddenly, there are great numbers of geese on our ponds. The one-year-olds and two-year-olds, which are not yet old enough to breed, return from Lake Alm, where they have been living quietly in the tranquil creeks and on the broad expanse of the lake. Some geese that have bred elsewhere also return. One of these is a female called Yksi, whose mate bears the name Lacchini, in honor of my friend Colonel Lacchini, who also maintains a goose colony. She breeds on a grassy island in Lake Chiem, easily 125 miles from Oberganslbach as the crow flies, and in the autumn she flies back to the Alm Valley with her offspring to spend the winter with us. There is a second family that returns regularly, whose breeding site we do not know. It is a time when there are many geese, much calling, and a great deal of excitement in the Alm Valley, since all the geese are affected by the migratory urge, even those that will not actually fly away. Although we know that many of them will not migrate, we always observe them with a certain anxiety, as if we could already see them moving off through the sky.

There were no wild geese in the Alm Valley before our arrival, with the possible exception of a few individuals passing through and stopping off for a rest. We ourselves saw only a few solitary bean geese in the valley after we settled there. One stayed on Lake Alm for a while in 1974, and a second, which suddenly appeared in September 1977 and attached itself to our own five bean geese, has been with us ever since. The latter was still bearing juvenile plumage when it arrived and had doubtless been separated from its parents by accident. The same could well have been true of the other individual.

We introduced the greylag geese into the Alm Valley. A great deal of work is necessary to create a colony of free-living geese, but success is certain as long as one does not shirk the labor. The first step in the establishment of a colony is the incubation of eggs: *omne vivum ex ovo* ("all life comes from the egg"). Despite many experiments, however, we have not found a fully reliable method of artificial incubation. We have had far better success with using domestic geese for brooding. But these creatures, rendered stupid by many years of domestication, are incapable of reliable incubation; they have lost the well-defined instinctive behavior patterns a wild goose exhibits, as discussed above. Left to themselves, the domestic geese do not take brooding pauses often enough, or, if they do, they will not always take a dip and frequently will return to the nest too soon or with dry feathers. When these geese are being used to hatch out wild goose eggs, they must be thrown off the nest at regular intervals—and remember that the domestic goose can deliver a nasty bite. The introduction of these artificial brooding pauses all too often procures one of us a painful blood blister on the hand. Also, the domestic goose must either be sprinkled with water or thrown into it so that she will carry enough moisture back to the nest. In addition, it is better if we turn the eggs ourselves; a brooding domestic goose cannot perform even this task reliably.

In fact, one cannot dispense altogether with the use of an artificial incubator, since, as I have said, an emerging gosling must immediately attach itself to a human foster parent as a necessary precondition to ensuring that it will settle in a specific place. That attachment is possible only if the goslings are cared for the moment they hatch—indeed, while they are hatching. As we have seen, social communication begins, through calls exchanged rather like questions and answers, even before the gosling hatches from the egg.

At the blunt end of the egg is the air chamber, which we know about from our breakfast eggs. Any sensible person will open an egg from the blunt end, because of the air cavity—though there are always a few heretics who open their eggs from the pointed end.

In Jonathan Swift's *Gulliver's Travels*, that difference of opinion led to a war in Lilliput.

Hatching begins when the gosling uses its beak to break through the membrane separating the air cavity from the rest of the egg's contents. Now the gosling breathes with its lungs for the first time. Previously, its supply of oxygen came from the blood circulating in the membranes of the egg. As soon as the gosling starts breathing with its lungs, it also begins to utter calls. When the egg becomes too cool the gosling produces plaintive single "lost piping" calls, and it responds with a two-part "greeting" call when a comforting reply is given from the outside. One never fails to be surprised to observe such a "conversation" taking place with an unbroken egg.

It takes several hours after that for the first hole to appear in the eggshell. The hole is, in fact, not "pecked" out, but results from outward pressure exerted by the egg tooth. In emerging from the egg, the gosling turns its body around the long axis of the egg while constantly pressing on the shell with the egg tooth. The egg tooth is a genuine tooth, the only one retained by birds as a heritage from their reptilian ancestral stock. Reptiles also have an egg tooth, which, like a bird's, grows not in the mouth but on the tip of the nose. An unhatched bird does not "peck" at the eggshell with its egg tooth; there is too little room to do that. Its head is inclined forward in a curious way, passing beneath one of the wings in such a manner that the forehead and upper part of the beak press against the external membrane and shell. Stretching the neck, which has powerful muscles, forces the egg tooth outward, breaking a small hole in the shell. At the same time the young bird is rotating slightly around the long axis of the egg, so that the egg tooth is always bringing pressure on a different part of the shell.

Hatching is not a single continuous process. After the first fracture has been made in the egg, the gosling typically will rest for a while. In addition, all hatching activity ceases during the night, probably because the mother is also resting then. Her help is limited during hatching, but it is nevertheless important.

This gosling is halfway through the laborious hatching process, having chipped its way around half of the blunt end of the egg. Its down feathers, still in their horny sheaths, can be clearly seen. By the end of the brooding period the originally white eggs have a dull, dirty yellow-brown appearance. That is the result of the egg's continual rubbing against the oily feathers of the mother, which is necessary for keeping the shell permeable to air. These particular eggs were incubated by domestic geese and then placed in an artificial incubator for the actual hatching.

When the gosling has finally created a complete ring of fractures around the blunt end of the egg (92), it pushes off the cap in one piece by stretching its neck (93). At this point it can thrust itself without difficulty out of the opening by stretching its legs (94).

Like most other down-covered hatchlings, the freshly hatched gosling at first appears to be damp (95), an impression that is given because in the egg the down feathers are covered with fine horny sheaths, to prevent them from unfolding. The sheaths dry and fall off soon after hatching, leaving only a fine dust, and the down feathers unfold to their full size (97). Then it is difficult to imagine how such a big gosling could have come from such a small egg. At this stage, the egg tooth is still clearly visible on the tip of the beak (96).

The newly hatched gosling retains a considerable amount of yolk in its digestive tract, which will keep it alive as long as two days. However, the gosling must learn what is edible in the outside world before its food reserve is exhausted. Almost as soon as they have left the nest, goslings begin to show interest in finding food. They peck at everything and, contrary to my initial expectation, show no instinctive preference for green objects. It is mainly small things that they peck at, and in doing so they show the complete motor patterns exhibited by full-grown geese, of tugging, biting off, and swallowing plants. But they must still learn to identify the objects that are appropriate for the motor patterns (98).

Human foster parents can help goslings to find appropriate food items by stabbing at them with a finger. One thing we noticed was that goslings led by human foster parents would plunge enthusiastically into puddles on a path or road and vigorously perform the behavior patterns of dabbling on the ground at the bottom of the puddle. They never did this in muddy natural ponds, only in pools of water on a pathway or in the road. It took a while before we realized what they were after. Geese have a muscular stomach with a tough, horny inner wall. With the aid of small stones that the goose swallows, this organ mills down the bird's

By stretching its neck, this hatchling has pushed away the cap of the egg. Soon it will escape from the rest of the shell by kicking its legs.

94
The gosling has just hatched, and for a
short while it lies exhausted from its
great exertions. However, it will soon
raise its head, attempt to creep into its
mother's plumage, and emit a soft greeting call in the direction of the first
source of sound it encounters.

95
A freshly hatched gosling, picked up in the hand, is not yet able to hold up its head or neck, and its tiny wings are still tightly held to its body.

96
The yellow egg tooth, used to crack open the shell, can be seen on the tip of the gosling's shiny black beak. Within a few days the egg tooth will drop off.

97
As a natural result of rubbing against the mother's feathers while burrowing beneath her, the gosling loses the horny sheaths from its feathers. This converts it from a damp and rather ugly creature to a fluffy, yellow-green ball of down feathers.

98
The young gosling is already able to perform all the grazing patterns of adult geese, but for the first few days it lacks strength to pull out grass stems and other small plants. This is not a serious problem, however, since the gosling can survive for about three days after hatching on the remaining contents of the yolk sac.

The goslings must be rubbed against the mother's plumage in order to become waterproof. This happens when they huddle under her body. Since hand-reared goslings are robbed of this possibility, they are often less water-proof than their wild counterparts, as is the case with the gosling shown here—wet feathers cling to its neck and wings.

fiber-rich food. Our goslings were attempting to find in the puddles suitable stones for their stomachs.

Our earlier batches of hand-reared goslings suffered somewhat from the problem that when they swam or bathed their down feathers did not remain as superbly waterproof as those of goslings reared by their own parents (99). The most obvious explanation seemed to be that our goslings' plumage lacked the oiling it would normally get when an offspring snuggles beneath its mother and rubs against her well-oiled feathers. We knew that the oil gland on the gosling's rump does not begin to function until a few weeks after hatching. Accordingly, we thought we could correct the deficiency in our hand-reared goslings by "milking" the rump gland of an adult goose and massaging the youngsters with the oily product we obtained. However, they suffered even more from wetting after this treatment. Only gradually did it dawn on us that the waterproofing of a gosling's plumage is due less to the oiliness of the mother's feathers than to the static electric charge produced when the offspring rubs its down feathers against the mother's belly plumage. That also led us to understand why geese and other water birds whose feathers have become somewhat permeable to water preen themselves so much (100). It is to restore the electric charge and with it the waterproofing of their feathers. Once we had grasped that, we began to rub our young goslings thoroughly with a silk cloth, and they became just as well waterproofed as any youngsters reared by their own parents.

Yet none of these measures is as vital for the well-being of a young greylag goose as its psychological care is. It has already been pointed out that communication between mother and offspring begins well before the gosling has broken its first hole in the eggshell. After hatching, the communication becomes more intensive and increasingly important. A few minutes after emerging from the egg, the gosling attempts to raise its head. As soon as it has done so, it can respond to a stimulus from the parental guardian not with greeting calls alone but with an accompanying display. That is, it raises its head and stretches its neck. Somewhat later, when visual orientation has begun to appear, the gosling directs the display toward the point from where it can hear calls or where it can see the guardian moving. In doing so, the gosling looks with concentrated attention in that direction, as if to imprint upon itself the guardian's image. That is particularly true when the guardian bends over the gosling from above and the latter inclines its head to stare up at him with one eye. The immediate impression given by this behavior is actually quite accurate. The gosling possesses innate information that, if translated into words, would read as follows: "Whoever responds to your lost piping is your mother; take careful note of her appearance."

This first round of communication between mother and offspring constitutes the vital process of *imprinting*, which can never be repeated or reversed. When the dialogue takes place between a gosling and a human being, even if only a few times, it subsequently becomes apparent that the juvenile innate behavior patterns of the freshly hatched gosling are permanently fixed on the human foster parent. I was to find out just how rigid the bond is with my very first greylag gosling. I took it out from under the domestic goose that had hatched it for just a few minutes and elicited the greeting response I have described. From then on, the gosling obstinately refused to accept the domestic goose as its mother; it could not be freed of the conviction that I was its mother.

In order to play their maternal role with complete success, foster parents must be prepared to devote their time exclusively to the adopted goslings for several weeks. The foster children cannot be left alone for a moment or they will immediately begin to "cry" in confusion. That is, they utter the so-called lost piping—an emergency signal to which their parents would respond at once. The human foster parent must do exactly the same or the goslings will become seriously neurotic—or at least will exhibit behavioral disturbances that render them unfit for a study of the social behavior of their species.

The enormous amount of time one must spend in close contact with the adopted goslings, if they are to be kept conscientiously in full mental health, obliges the scientist involved to live for long

101
*"Hare's foot" is a food item particularly
favored by the young goslings.*

periods under natural conditions. The foster parent shares in all the
little joys and sorrows of the goslings. One has to smile in sympathy
with them when they tread on a patch of nettles and pipe in
distress, or share their pleasure when they utter calls of "content-
ment" while feeding on the flowers of the "hare's foot" (101),
an attractive plant whose Latin name I am sorry to admit we do
not know.

In good weather, with the sun shining warmly down, being a
substitute mother for waterfowl hardly seems like work (102, 103).
On the other hand, anyone can see that when it is pouring rain
it is a major undertaking to spend day after day, around the clock,
with young geese. It is evident from photograph 104 how
raindrops tumble off the plumage of the young geese, which is
much more waterproof than the foster parent's raincoat. Geese
are very well protected by nature against the weather. They are not
bothered at all by rainstorms, though if it hails they will lift their
beaks toward the sky so that the hailstones hit their skulls at a
tangent rather than straight down (105).

In our alpine valley the weather often changes abruptly, and
a rainbow, as depicted in photograph 106, is a very welcome
harbinger of better weather.

The duties of a foster parent include providing the goslings
with the necessary orientation. For this, long excursions must be
conducted. It is the most strenuous and exacting, but also the most
rewarding, part of the year for the human substitute parents of
young geese. I had intended from the outset to make our young
geese familiar not only with our ponds at Oberganslbach, but also
with the rest of the large area of the Alm Valley that had been
placed at our disposal. It was obviously impossible to travel such
long distances with the little goslings, and so we had to hold back
our geography lessons until they were large enough to cope with the
trips without overexertion. In practice, it meant that the only time
we could make the longer excursions was the period just before
fledging.

Moving out from Oberganslbach was always a drawn-out,

The most important quality required in a goose observer is patience. Anyone who finds it too boring to sit with geese for hours at a time and participate in their daily routine is not really cut out for this kind of work.

rather boring episode, since geese are extremely conservative creatures and are averse to venturing into unknown terrain. The resident foster parents of our hand-reared flocks, with me as a kind of "uncle" to them all, had to spend a great deal of time calling the geese and then waiting for them to make up their minds to leave Oberganslbach behind and seek out new pathways. Once that was over with, however, and the young geese found themselves in unknown territory for the first time, they followed us eagerly and faithfully on foot. If they lagged the least bit behind, they would immediately give distress calls. They were anxious, of course, in this new situation, and the familiar human caretakers represented for them the only trustworthy and reassuring things around. For that very reason, excursions into new areas produce a powerful bonding. The effect can also be exploited by a person with a new dog. Anyone who acquires a young dog that is actually somewhat old for the establishment of an ideal master-dog relationship can do no better than to take the dog for long walks over unknown terrain. Dogs are by nature predisposed to travel considerable distances. They greatly enjoy running, and the farther and faster that their master goes with them, the better it is for establishing the desired bond.

In the latter respect geese are different from dogs. Once we had lured the flock into an unknown area and they had begun to walk after us eagerly and obediently, almost at a normal human walking pace, we made the mistake a few times of forcing them to travel longer distances quite rapidly. Human beings are, after all, impatient creatures. But we soon noticed that after their fear of the unknown had been exploited in this way the geese would simply refuse to leave Oberganslbach the next time. They seemed to be saying, "Once, but never again." That was one of our first indications that it is unwise to foist unpleasant experiences on geese and, more important, that they are less ready to accept severe "frustration" than human children are. We had to learn to walk at the geese's speed with our flock and to avoid paths on which they

103
On a hot summer day, the task of leading a flock of young geese through the beautiful countryside would doubtless appear to any onlooker to be an unmitigated pleasure. But it can be an irritating and demanding undertaking, since the needs of the goslings must be met as and when they arise.

104
When it rains constantly for days or even weeks, leading a flock of geese becomes a really strenuous task. For the geese, on the other hand, such weather is just as acceptable as sunshine, and they still insist on remaining in the open from dawn to dusk.

In a driving rain or a hailstorm, the geese lay their feathers flat and stretch their heads high, reducing to a minimum the body surface exposed to the assault of the weather. This behavior also keeps hailstones from pounding straight down on the roof of the skull.

After a violent summer storm a rainbow often appears over the cloud-bedecked valley.

showed uneasiness. For instance, they would try to avoid going through dense undergrowth or walking for any length of time on stony pathways that hurt their soft feet.

From time to time we would stop to rest, or we would take longer breaks at a spot that was pleasant for the geese, offering them tasty grazing plants, easily accessible water, and a wide-ranging view.

Through these techniques, which we learned from the geese themselves, we induced them to follow us over greater and greater distances. Then, after they were able to fly properly, we became really ambitious. We decided to set out with them on a trip all the way to Lake Alm. We assumed that our foster children, which had taken to the air to follow us part of the way on previous outings, would then be able to fly back to Oberganslbach from Lake Alm. They were trained for that to the extent that we would run upstream ahead of them—faster than they were inclined to walk—and call them from some distance away. In response, they would fly after us, swooping just above the surface of the river Alm (107). Afterward they were regularly rewarded for their compliance with a lengthy rest break and with favorite plant foods that I picked for them on the way.

On the big day, we left Oberganslbach very early in the morning (108). It is remarkably tiring for a human being to cover a long distance at the walking pace of a flock of geese, which never exceeds a speed of 1.25 miles an hour. The rest periods we had to include for the geese were therefore just as welcome to us (109, 110, 111). When the weather was good, these recuperation pauses were most enjoyable, especially the long midday rest.

It is part of the regular schedule of a goose's day that a bath is taken around noon. Immediately after bathing, it is an "obligation" for a goose to preen its feathers carefully and restore their oil coating. While they are in the process of performing that important activity, geese cannot be induced to move by anything less than brute force. Even the most obedient young geese will stubbornly refuse to follow their human foster parents if the latter attempt to depart from the natural schedule of things and lead them away.

*To lead the geese away from familiar
territory, their human companions must
set off "in a closed flock." Travel
through unknown terrain represents a
considerable hazard to the geese.*

109
During a break on one of their walks the young geese nibble inquisitively at their foster mother's trouser legs—already badly damaged by such treatment!

111
On our walks, we collect favored food plants, such as thistles, so that we can pamper the geese during rest periods. In the center of this photograph can be seen Selma, who grew up to become so notorious, and two of her brothers when they were only two months old.

110
When they are out on excursions, the geese like to take extended breaks in order to dabble in the shallows by the riverbank, or eat favorite food plants collected by their human companions along the way. In this case, they are eating horsetail especially plucked for them.

112
To get to Lake Alm we have to cross the river repeatedly. With the racing water and the coarse gravel on the riverbed to contend with, it is no easy task, and from time to time one of us will fall in the water. In warm weather that is not too disastrous, but when the weather is bad it is particularly uncomfortable to continue walking in soaking wet clothes.

113
A midday rest in the rain is hardly an enjoyable occasion for the human participants, but the geese are not in the least perturbed. Here, they are indulging in one of their favorite habits, nibbling at their foster mother's rainproof clothing. The family in the background has already drifted off to sleep.

Real goose parents, of course, could never commit such an error, since they would have taken a dip themselves and would therefore be in equal need of a careful preening. It is also an inviolable custom to follow the preening with a fairly long nap.

The human goose parents nap even more soundly than their charges. To be sure, they begin the day's work at cockcrow (the geese are always up by then), and they finish at nightfall, when their foster children fall sound asleep. But since my co-workers have other tasks to perform after that, it is inevitable that they eventually build up a considerable sleep deficit, which must be compensated for by a siesta. Nothing is cozier than such a siesta shared by man and beast. The trilling call young geese utter as they fall asleep is the sweetest lullaby imaginable, and the shared repose of wild animals and civilized people in the midst of nature has an almost sacred quality. That makes it all the more sobering and infuriating when, as is typical of the Alm Valley, a raincloud abruptly appears and pours a cold shower over the resting bodies. The birds and the humans react in quite different ways. Only the latter wake up cursing and reach for their raincoats; the geese, in contrast, have no need for such protection and continue to sleep undisturbed (113).

On this excursion, as with any move upstream, we followed the course of the river Alm, since, as we know, shortcuts are unpleasant for the geese. Flat riverbanks suitable for the geese are found sometimes on one side of the Alm and sometimes on the other. We repeatedly had to wade across the rushing water, and in the process it was easy to stumble and fall (112). We had become so attuned to the perceptual world of our geese that we ourselves found it downright unpleasant to have to take a shortcut along a forest road (117), however beautiful the surroundings. The pale flowers in the background are foxglove (*Digitalis grandiflora* Linnaeus, 114); the river is lined with more modest blossoms, such as those of the small sandwort (*Moehringia ciliata* Linnaeus, 115)

If we use pathways away from the water, the geese are very attentive, keeping continuous watch around them and hurrying straight back toward the Alm at the earliest opportunity. Once they are separated from the water, the slightest alarm is enough to make them take to the air. When that happens, they usually fly back to Oberganslbach, thus reducing all our efforts to nothing. In this picture, one can see the tense watchfulness of the geese in their flattened neck feathers, their erect necks, and their sideways gaze into the forest.

and the tiny harebell (*Campanula rotundiflora* Linnaeus, 116).

Both the geese and their human companions were quite tired when we finally reached the point where the river Alm emerges from Lake Alm. Our boat (118) awaited us there, and that unfamiliar object at first aroused the mistrust of our foster children. Since it was also their first sight of a large body of water, they were in an anxious mood to begin with. As with many herd-living animals, when geese are subject to pronounced uneasiness the herd drive predominates over their usual aversion to strangers. It can be seen in photograph 119 how four families of young greylag geese, which had been hand-reared by four different foster parents, thronged together in a single dense flock. This was something they had never done "at home" on the ponds where they were reared.

It took some time for the geese to become accustomed to the boat, despite the fact that their four foster parents and I, the familiar "uncle" of the flock, were all sitting in it and calling to them. But finally they followed the boat in a tightly packed flock (120). Although they later grew used to the boat, to this day they will follow it only when they know its human occupants. If strangers are sitting in the boat, the geese become very frightened, almost more so than when confronted with a different boat. On this first day, we led the flock to the northern end of the lake, near its outlet, where reeds and peat moss cover the marshland. Here one finds that exquisite little insect-eating plant known as the sundew (*Drosera rotundifolia* Linnaeus).

On that first excursion to Lake Alm with the geese, they covered large parts of the way on the wing, although, as noted, they always flew low along the river course. However, the final stretch leading into Lake Alm had to be completed through dense woodland, since the banks of the river at that point are far too steep for us to walk along.

It was one o'clock in the afternoon when we at last reached Lake Alm with our goose flock. We had set out from home at seven in the morning, and it had taken us six hours to walk to our goal. Now a difficult decision faced us. In order to reward the geese for

114
The yellow foxglove (Digitalis grandiflora L.) blooms in clearings and on open patches along the path.

115
The tiny sandwort (Moehringia ciliata L.) grows on the banks of the river Alm and on the gravel flats of the lake.

116
The tiny harebell (Campanula rotundiflora L.) blooms on the meadows lining the riverbank.

118
When we first arrived at Lake Alm, the geese were glad to see a large expanse of water again but at the same time were rather afraid of their new surroundings. As a result, they stuck closely to us.

119
Our young geese were encountering the lake for the first time. Never before had they been out swimming on such a large body of water, nor had they seen such depths. They were rather unsettled at first, for the water is so clear that every detail of the lake bed can be seen. They therefore kept close together and swam rapidly alongside the boat with their necks stretched alertly upward.

120
Once the geese had become more familiar with the lake and the boat, they swam behind us in single file and would even fly some distance to join us. However, they responded in this way only to our boat; strange boats were immediately recognized and avoided.

121
The swampy islands of Lake Alm are much more enjoyable for the geese, which like to graze and dabble there, than they are for us. With every step in the peat moss a puddle forms around one's foot, and even an air mattress rapidly becomes soaked.

their exertions, we needed to spend as long a time as possible with them in a place they found agreeable. That meant staying with them until evening at a beautiful spot on the southern shore of the lake (121). We knew well enough that we could motivate our geese to fly by imitating flight calls and takeoff movements and could then induce them to actually take to the air by running a short way in front of them. But we did not know whether the geese would merely circle a few times and land alongside us again, or whether they would take the route back to their usual sleeping site, as we hoped. If the geese did not do as we expected, we faced the prospect of walking back downstream with them, a trip of up to seven hours. Worse, if night fell while we were on the way, we would have to make camp and pass the night in the open with the geese. For me, with my clothes still wet, that would have been a somewhat hazardous proposition, and I began to wonder whether I could use it as an excuse, should one be necessary, for perfidiously abandoning my colleagues and my geese. A fine piece of brinkmanship was involved. The later we waited before inciting the geese to fly off, the greater was the probability that they would be in a mood to retire to sleep and would therefore seek out their customary sleeping quarters. At the same time, the later we waited the more unpleasant became the prospect of returning home on foot.

In the event, we waited until five-thirty in the evening, a time of day when geese typically are highly motivated to fly. We performed our flight-incitement ceremony (always an exhilarating sight for spectators), and our geese promptly responded. They flew once entirely around the lake, and we watched anxiously as they passed above us, making sure not to utter a single sound that might have attracted them to return. The flock circled the lake once more, and as the geese passed above us for the second time we saw that they had gained considerable height. We watched with relief, but at the same time somewhat anxiously, as they disappeared into the mountain cleft leading downstream.

Sitting by a hut alongside our ponds at Oberganslbach were a few of our team who had remained behind. We had been unable

122
The geese arrive over Oberganslbach high in the sky after flying from Lake Alm. Even before they reach our ponds they utter loud distance calls, and their wing beats are stilled as they glide in over the final stretch.

123
The geese circle over our heads a few times and then land very close to the huts.

In this young goose, the feathers of the juvenile plumage can easily be distinguished from those of the adult. At the ends of the light, pointed juvenile feathers sit yellow down feathers, while the dark, blunt feathers with the pale borders are recognizable as belonging to the adult plumage.

125
The swallowtail gentian (Gentiana
pannonica *SCOP*) *blooms in the sparse
forest during late summer.*

126
The man-high marsh thistles (Cirsium
pallustra *L.*) *bloom when the young
geese have acquired their full flying
powers.*

to tell them exactly when we would send the geese flying back from the lake. Therefore they were both happy and relieved when they saw our flock of young geese make a timely appearance high in the sky, fly along the valley (122), swoop down, and finally land firmly beside the hut (123). After their tiring day, all the geese went to sleep immediately. On the goose in the photograph, one can easily distinguish the older, lighter, and pointed feathers of the juvenile plumage—the tips of which not so long ago bore the last of the down feathers—from the new, darker, and more truncated feathers of the adult plumage (124).

Late summer is perhaps the most magnificent time of year in the valleys of the northern Alps; there are more clear, sunny days than at any other time. One can almost forget that autumn is not far off when one sees the late blossoms of such flowers as the swallowtail gentian (*Gentiana pannonica* SCOP, 125) and the marsh thistle (*Cirsium pallustra* Linnaeus, 126). On clear September days the landscape still has the appearance of high summer (127). However, the geese now become a cause of concern to their human foster parents as their motivation to fly off increases. Since human beings unfortunately cannot fly off with them, we are sometimes left standing around forlorn and anxious.

Suddenly one morning the mountains are covered with snow (130), the leaves turn an autumn yellow (128), and the spiders' webs are coated with pearls of dew at daybreak (129). Then our wild geese become very restless indeed. We also become restless, although we know from experience that the geese will not fly away for good, and that even if some of them do go astray the chances are good that they will turn up again one day. There are few events that please us so much as the return of a long-lost greylag goose. We half wish that some of our geese would meet up with the wild greylag goose population of Lake Neusiedler, so that our colony would adopt from them the tradition of migrating down to the Danube delta. We are well aware how dangerous such a migration can be, but we would nevertheless be glad to have our geese resemble their wild counterparts in migratory behavior, too. So when our

127
The warm, sunny days of late summer and early autumn on Lake Alm are particularly delightful. When the dawn mist has cleared, the green mirror of the lake surface can be seen lying beneath a radiant blue sky. Over the mountains, and there alone, can be seen the typical wisps of the föhn cloud.

130
On autumn evenings, as night falls, the geese fly from the Auingerhof mill to their sleeping sites on Lake Alm. Before settling down to sleep, they dabble a short while in the swampy lake bed by the shore.

128
In autumn the leaves of the maple turn bright yellow.

129
In the morning, dew hangs glistening on the spiders' webs.

beloved geese fly high above us uttering their migratory chorus, we stand by, way down on the earth, and watch with mixed feelings (131).

At this time of year I am always reminded of something that remains firmly fixed in my mind even though it happened almost seventy years ago. I am sure I had not started going to school and could not yet read. While out walking in the water meadows of the Danube, I had disobediently run ahead, against the wishes of my anxious mother and my even more anxious Aunt Hedwig, and was standing in a small clearing near the Danube. I heard above me some peculiar metallic calls and then saw, way up in the sky, a flock of wild geese heading downstream. Human emotions develop early and remain unchanged for life. I can still relive today exactly what I felt at that moment. I did not know where the birds were flying, *but I wanted to migrate with them.* I was filled with a romantic, chest-expanding, heart-bursting longing to travel. This, to my certain knowledge, was also the first time in my life when I felt an uncontrollable urge to express myself artistically. For my age, I had a fair talent for drawing, and my mother encouraged me by making sure there was always a large table I could use, as well as colored chalk, an unlimited supply of paper, and a large biscuit tin full of assorted colored pencils.

After that experience near the river, I frequently drew and painted geese—which led me even at that early age to a bitter realization: in the world of art, tripe inevitably results when the artist's enthusiasm outruns the level of his artistic ability. There happens to be one writer I know of whose artistic talent does justice to the romantic aura of migratory birds and who portrays their precarious and heroic existence with great skill: Selma Lagerlöf. I came to know her book *Young Nils Holgersson's Journey with the Wild Geese* only after I had had my rousing experience with the migrating geese. At first I was not at all interested in the book, because my lively imagination interpreted the title to mean that Nils Holgersson's voyage was on a train, with the wild geese in cages. I foresaw that the geese were going to be slaughtered, in a manner I had unfortunately already witnessed in my parent's home. Eventually,

On stormy days the migratory urge is
awakened in our geese, and they fly for
hours in the dark autumn sky above the
mountains before eventually returning
to us. On such long-distance flights, they
always take up the typical V formation.

In autumn the goose flock moves from
Oberganslbach to the gravel flats by the
institute building on Lake Alm. At first
they are somewhat unsure of themselves
and do not dare to land immediately.
To induce them to come in to land, we
run in front of them and stoop abruptly.

though, I realized that that was not what happened in Selma Lagerlöf's book. In due course, the story was read to me, and that is how I can date these occurrences accurately. I learned to read early, before I started to go to school, and therefore all this must have taken place prior to 1909.

For me, that childhood romance is inextricably linked with the time when the geese migrate. It is reawakened whenever I see our wild geese fly over high above me, and a childhood dream comes true when I call to them and they magically fly down toward me (132). The photograph shows Sybille Kalas crouching rapidly to induce the geese to land in a particular spot. When the geese are flying past way up in the sky, the picture we see is roughly what is shown in the next photograph (133). On the other hand, our house must look to the flying geese rather as it does in a photograph taken from a high mountain peak (134). We must seem small indeed to the geese, and even if the sound of our voices carries well in the air, it is undoubtedly quite weak by the time it reaches them. The contrast in these two situations always makes me conscious of the truly wonderful nature of our familiarity with wild birds. At one instant the geese are flying past among the clouds, and at the next they are so close that the intimate contact obliges one to take photographs purely for the pleasure of it, as Sybille has done (135, 136, 137). The last photograph, in particular, clearly shows how much fun she had taking it.

The dangers migratory birds repeatedly face are underlined by the fact that during these long flights there are always a few individuals that go astray. We do not know whether they deliberately attach themselves to strange flocks or whether (as is more likely) they simply lose their way. In any case, one is never without a certain feeling of anxiety when watching a goose flock disappear high in the sky, the sound of their calls gradually trailing off.

But the autumn migratory period is not only a time of loss; often there are gratifying reunions as well. As I have said, we watch for the return of certain goose pairs that have bred elsewhere. When they come back to the Alm Valley in autumn, they bring their new offspring with them, and we cannot wait to see whether the

133
The geese fly past high in the sky.

134
This view of the institute from the neighboring Kasberg gives an idea of what the geese see when they fly past. In the center of the picture can be seen Lake Alm and the gravel flats on which the geese like to land.

135
Shortly before touching down on the ground, the geese thrust their feet forward and brake themselves with powerful wing beats.

136
It is always a magnificent experience when the geese arrive in the sky, begin to circle, and then land alongside us with a flurry of wing beats.

new additions will pair off with any of our resident geese and so remain with us. Our photograph (138) shows the arrival in autumn 1976 of the Yksi family, which had bred in Bavaria.

Less poetic, but in its way particularly touching, is the return of stray geese by train. In the autumn, tame, hand-reared geese that have gone astray often will seek sanctuary with unfamiliar people, and we will be notified of their whereabouts via the bird research station at Radolfzell. One of the most encouraging cases was that of the brothers Xaver and Valentin, which had been hand-reared in 1973 at the Max Planck Institute, in Seewiesen, while we were still located there. They dropped in on some delightful people living near Landshut, in Lower Bavaria, who kindly notified us. We wrote back asking them to try to catch the two ganders and send them by train to the institute in Seewiesen, where we would collect them at the earliest opportunity. However, we forgot to tell these obliging people that it is possible to catch two geese only if they are tackled simultaneously. One tame goose will allow itself to be grasped and carried off, but a second one, on seeing this, will be warned off and will never allow itself to be caught. Our friends near Landshut caught just Xaver, enclosed him in a crate, and sent him to Starnberg, the nearest station to Seewiesen. Valentin had disappeared. But even before Xaver in his crate arrived in Starnberg and the institute in Seewiesen was notified, he landed—tired, but otherwise in immaculate condition—under his own steam in Oberganslbach. Obviously he had not lost his sense of direction! When his brother had disappeared during the stopover near Landshut, it had made him unhappy with the area and he had decided to fly back home.

It proved well worth our while to bring back any stray geese that were reported seen in far-flung places, even when it involved a certain amount of trouble and expense. These geese, which had usually been through some harrowing experiences, consistently became more closely attached to us and their home base after they were brought back. One is almost tempted to talk of "gratitude." On one occasion, when Sybille was collecting a crate containing a lost gander from the express parcel office at the nearest railway

137

*On fine autumn days, we enjoy the sun's
last warm rays along with the geese,
which have gathered nearby for their
midday rest. In the picture Alma's legs
provide a worthy frame for our institute.*

138

*On a stormy October day, Yksi and
Lacchini suddenly arrived, to land on
Lake Alm with the offspring they had
reared on Lake Chiem. They approached
very watchfully and hesitantly, and only
after a long period of scanning their
surroundings carefully did they begin
to gabble in a relaxed way and to feed
on the scattered grain.*

station and asked an official about it, she was answered by loud calls and greeting cackles in the distance; the goose in the crate had recognized her voice.

The geese that have bred elsewhere might fly several hundred miles from their brooding sites to the Alm Valley. In contrast, our resident geese fly only a few miles in the strictest sense, since they transfer no farther than from Oberganslbach to the Auingerhof mill. As I said before, sometimes the geese move across even before the goose caretakers have transferred from their little hut to the research station building. But the latter are thankful for the small hint that it is time to move, as the weather can be very cold at this time of year.

Autumn gives way to winter's reign, and that often happens earlier than we would like in the Alm Valley. As soon as the snow lies thick on the ground, the geese, which until then have spent their time on the meadows surrounding the research station, restrict their activities to the vicinity of the river, usually staying on the sandbanks, where they can find food (139, 140). They have become more settled; the period of migratory restlessness has passed, and there is not much of interest for us to observe in their behavior. Nevertheless, we spend as much time with them as we can, in order to maintain the trusting relationship they have with us. In even the warmest of clothing, we feel the cold far more than the geese do and can only wonder at the efficiency of their isolating plumage, which is permeable to air but impermeable to both water and cold.

The sandbanks in the Alm do not provide adequate protection against foxes, and so the geese fly upstream at dusk to pass the night on the ice-free surface of Lake Alm. With the first light of day our geese come flying back downstream, a distance of about five miles. Since, as explained earlier, they stay at the height of their elevated takeoff point during the flight, they are well up in the sky when they arrive at Oberganslbach, and they dive down to land in a roaring plunge. When there is heavy frost the geese do not walk around much, and to keep their feet warm they often stand at the edge of a sandbank in the relatively warm water of the river Alm (143).

139
In winter the flock is very close-knit. Many rivalries and enmities now seem forgotten.

184

The geese remain at their feeding site by our house until late in the evening, and then abruptly take to the air in a tight-packed flock to disappear into the mist, flying just above the surface of the water.

141
As the first harbinger of spring, one can find the yellow-green flowers of the opposite-leaved golden saxifrage (Chrysosplenium oppositifolium L.) on the banks of streams and in other humid places.

142
The large spring snowflake (Leucojum vernum L.) blooms in the damp surroundings of the alder forest near Lake Alm as soon as the snow has vanished.

I would not want to live in a country where the four seasons are not sharply distinct from each other. When someone, such as one of the members of our research team, lives in close contact with nature and her living creatures, that person learns to love every one of the seasons as they follow their course. How beautiful the cold, clear winter days are in the Alm Valley, with the sun lighting the mountain crests, shadows in the valley, and a fine mist hanging over the water. What a magnificent sight it is to look through a hole in the cloud layer covering the dark and gloomy valley and see the oblique rays of the morning sun spotlighting a flock of geese flying above. And how dramatic it is when the geese break through the mist and appear under the cloud layer to land on a sandbank, sending up a swirl of frosty snow in the draft from their wings.

There is still heavy frost about, but the days are somewhat longer, the sun shines more strongly, and the geese are becoming more active. While autumn arrives slowly and stealthily in the Alm Valley, spring often appears with striking suddenness. One evening there will be föhn weather (144); the south wind will come blustering over the "Dead Mountain" into the valley and the snow will begin to melt. As soon as a few snow-free patches appear on the ground, the first spring flowers emerge, such as the opposite-leaved golden saxifrage (*Chrysosplenium oppositifolium* Linnaeus, 141) and the large spring snowflake (*Leucojum vernum* Linnaeus, 142). For the geese, that marks the onset once again of a period of excitation, of love and jealousy. For the human observer, too, it is the beginning of another spell of excitement and exertion, when it is impossible to observe and record as much as one would like. But it is also a time of hope. For it is the period when social mobility, pair modification, and other interesting aspects of social behavior can be expected. Now the research worker must get up especially early and be continually on duty. Experience has taught us that most of the events of greatest importance to our research take place in early spring. It is a time when we look forward to new discoveries and, no less, to many new goose families.

On bitter-cold winter days, the geese
stand in shallow water to keep their feet
warm. The vapor rising from the water
crystallizes on the trees lining the banks
to form a thick layer of hoarfrost.

There is still snow on the ground, but it
dwindles with every passing day. Hoarfrost has long since vanished, and a
warm föhn wind rushes through the
valley.

Postscript

As I said in the foreword to this book, I have made no attempt to provide here a scientifically cohesive description of the life of the greylag goose. That task is reserved for a quite different undertaking, an extensive monograph. What I have written here is merely an exposition to accompany the photographs compiled by Sybille Kalas—in fact, little more than a report of how the photographs came to be taken. The real story contained in the book is told by the photographs themselves. For whom is this story intended? Who is it that we hope and believe will absorb the story and understand the message it conveys?

Far too much of civilized mankind today is alienated from nature. Most people seldom encounter anything but lifeless, man-made things in their daily lives and have lost the capacity to understand living things or to interact with them. That loss helps explain why mankind as a whole exhibits such vandalism toward the living world of nature that surrounds us and makes our way of life possible. It is an important and worthy undertaking to try to restore the lost contact between human beings and the other living organisms of our planet. In the final analysis, the success or failure of such a venture will determine whether or not mankind destroys itself along with all the other living beings on earth.

People who have worked hard all day and in general tend to be stressed are not inclined to read alarming books, no matter how incontrovertibly accurate they are, warning of the dangers—books by such authors as Rachel Carson, Aldous Huxley, the Meadows team, and many others. Nobody wants to listen to penitential preaching after working hours, and warnings to save energy, to use less fuel oil, and generally to cut back on extravagance are unwelcome. Unfortunately, it is part of human nature to regard as a burden the need to do good. But people can respond to beauty when they are tired. Just as the pharmacist gives bitter pills a sugar coating, it will perhaps be possible through beauty to inspire overworked people who are alienated from nature with a sense of what is good and of their duty to protect and preserve nature's living things.

We believe the greylag goose is a particularly apt messenger to carry that appeal to a large urban public. Of the many animal species relatively familiar to most of us, there is only one whose behavior has a greater attraction for humans than that of the greylag goose—the dog. My father, who was a great dog lover, paid his greatest tribute to the geese when he once said, "After the dog, the greylag goose is the most suitable animal for association with human beings." Of course that applies to other wild goose species as well, but my father was familiar only with the greylag. The family and social life of wild geese exhibits an enormous number of striking parallels with human behavior. Let no one think it is misleading anthropomorphism to say so; we have learned, systematically and thoroughly, to avoid such errors in our work. We are, however, convinced by considerations relating to the theory of knowledge that higher animals are capable of subjective experience and that they can know happiness and sadness in much the same way as we do. When I return from a trip and my dogs scratch uncontrollably at the finish of my car before I can get out, and then tear at my clothing, I *know* that they are happy about my return, and also that there is little difference in the way I would show my happiness over the return of a long-lost friend. I will go a step further and say that anyone who knows dogs and has lived with them, but who *cannot* share in their happiness, is simply not a normal human being. Indeed, I would doubt that such a person was capable of sharing the feelings of his fellow-men.

Perhaps this book, through the attractiveness of its pictures—which are genuine factual documentation—will show the reader that there are other creatures besides ourselves that have a highly developed family and social life. I have mentioned the dog as an example that is familiar to most of us, but other animals also have a capacity for happiness and deep sadness, for love and attachment, for lasting bonds of genuine friendship. We hope a recognition of that will help to provoke sympathetic readers to clamor for the effective protection of nature and her animals.

Nothing could be further from my intention than to treat animals as a moralistic example to man, in the manner of Aesop or La Fontaine. The story "*Maître Corbeau sur un arbre perché*" ("Master Crow Perched in a Tree") has always annoyed me, if only because the stupid wretch drops the cheese in order to speak. No real crow would do that; the crow has a capacious laryngeal pouch under its tongue in which it can store objects when it must open its beak, and if an object is too large to be stored there, the crow will hold it firmly under one foot. I knew that at the age of six, when I had to learn the fable by heart—I still remember it word for word.

Animals have no sense of moral responsibility. Everything they do is a product of natural inclination, and their behavior is never guided by an anticipation of possible consequences that could harm their family or social group. But these natural inclinations are such that, with rare exceptions, an animal will reliably arrive at what is good, just as if a sense of responsible anticipation had dictated its actions. Animals do not *need* a sense of moral responsibility, since under natural conditions their inclinations lead them to what is *right*. In fact, human beings have many similar natural inclinations! But civilized people are often prevented by rational moral considerations from, say, treating their children as natural inclination would dictate. They are inhibited from cuddling and kissing them when they are well behaved and lovable, and from giving them a well-earned smack when they are naughty. That is not to mention the criminal nonsense that goes on in so-called anti-authoritarian education. Another area in which rational moral dictates mislead civilized man is the pace at which we work. Diligence is undoubtedly a virtue, just as laziness is a vice. But when a sense of duty drives us to undertake more work than we can accomplish without damaging our health, diligence becomes a regrettable vice, like any other form of excess.

One thing the geese can teach us by their example, in a manner not far removed from that of La Fontaine's fables, is how to relax and rest. I have said that the resting and sleeping calls of young geese represent the most beautiful and most effective lullaby I know. No matter how shallow the sleep of these wild birds is, or how alert their warning senses (particularly their fine hearing, which responds even in the deepest sleep), they are able to sink fully relaxed into sleep in a way that seems, among humans, to be confined to childhood. Let us end this book with a few pictures that show their beautiful relaxtion at its best!